GETTING YOUR FOOT
IN THE
EDITORIAL DOOR

Thomas A. Noton

A
TCW MARKETING GROUP BOOK

A TCW Marketing Group Book
Printed in the United States.
Copyright © 1983 Christian Horizons
Unlimited, Inc., all rights reserved.

TCW Marketing Group
P.O. Box 5650
Lakeland, FL 33803

ISBN-0-910459-00-2

Library of Congress Catalog Card
Number 83-72492

All artwork by Cindy Deaton

GETTING YOUR FOOT IN THE EDITORIAL DOOR

Thomas A. Noton

A step-by-step method of understanding and approaching editors and publishers.

DEDICATION

To Dr. Lew, Wanda, Louella, Stephen and Brent ... for your belief in our pursuit of writing excellence and your support of that cause.

A VERY SPECIAL NOTE
OF THANKS TO:

My wife, Bobbie, who has supported my writing habit for many years without complaint. You have been more than my mate, my friend, my love, my prodding, you've been a true wife. Thank you for success, as we measure it.

ACKNOWLEDGEMENTS

Bobbie (my wife)
Gary (my right arm)
Sandy (my secretary)
The Millers & The Fears (my board)
Karen (my editor)
Cindy (my artist)
Sally (my aid)
Charette (my encouragement)
Our many subscribers and supports (my reason)

SPECIAL THANKS TO:

Velma
Marlene
John
Patti
and to Dr. Dennis Hensley for his input.

. . . and Aggie (my friend)

i

FOREWARD

Getting Your Foot in the Editorial Door

We writers have nothing to lose. Sometimes, though, we feel everything is against us. Not only do we have too little time and never enough sympathy from nonwriters, we also live with the fear of rejection of ogre editors in mythical publishing houses.

But, I repeat, we writers have nothing to lose. The act of writing itself is great gain. It sharpens our insight, polishes our reasoning skills and leaves us with a sense of getting deeper into life than so many others around us.

"That's fine," you say, "but I want to be published."

I don't blame you. We all do. That's why Tom Noton wrote this book.

I just wish he had written it sooner. It would have saved me a lot of work! Many manuscripts with potential crossed my editorial desk, but I didn't have time to tell the authors how to mine the nuggets from all the ore in their manuscripts. And I certainly didn't have time to do the mining myself.

As a result, these potential books and articles were never published and many authors continued to be rejected. *Getting Your Foot in the Editorial Door* could have changed that.

As an editor and publisher, Tom Noton writes with inside knowledge of the industry. As a fine author himself, he identifies with writers everywhere. This book will help writers give editors and publishers what they want — "high-grade" material with easy access.

Of course, Tom is not perfect. In our times together discussing writing I've detected something that borders on obsession in his life.

Obsession is a malady I've seen often, especially in my capacity as an editor. It seems many writers are obsessed with their subject matter, blindly believing it to be the most important piece of hieroglyphics since Moses brought the tablets down from Mount Sinai.

Tom's obsession is different, however — and, to my way of thinking, unique. He is obsessed with helping writers improve their craft and actually become published. He loves the language, loves the writing profession, and loves people.

I frankly believe this book is an extension of Tom's obsession. It leads potential authors out of their fears that they will never be published and guides them to the correct publishing path.

Part I of the book quickly removes some of the perplexities from the art of writing, giving practical tips to improve your craft. And you will also learn how to satisfy editorial needs. (If there is no need for what you've written — no matter how well it's done — it won't get published.)

Part I might just open your eyes to new fields of writing, too.

So . . . you read Part I, practice what it says, and now want to be published. "How do I get it to the editor's desk?" you ask. "Should I try the sneaky approach and send my manuscript to the editor in an envelope marked 'personal,' having in bold print the return address of the local IRS office?"

Well, I'm sure this and other methods have been used to bypass normal editorial channels. But my suggestion is that you read the rest of *Getting Your Foot in the Editorial Door* instead.

Tom Noton next supplies unique observations from editors' and publishers' points of view. He helps you see through their eyes, then demonstrates how you can get your material directly to them. No more receiving a rejection slip from the front-office secretary who didn't consider your manuscript important enough to move into the editorial channels.

Getting Your Foot in the Editorial Door even discusses agents and such things as "vanity" publishers. Tom Noton lists their strengths and gives important warnings about some of their short-comings.

Getting Your Foot in the Editorial Door does not have magic formulas. Tom Noton does not guarantee that every writer will be published. He doesn't even say that writing is easy or that you will become an instant success.

What he does do is take the mystery out of the writing process and leave you with sound steps toward becoming published.

True, we writers have nothing to lose by writing,

even if we're never published. But it sure is nice to share our writing with others. And this readable book shows us how.

John D. Boneck
President, Promise Publishers, Inc.

PREFACE

As an author, editor and publisher, I've seen the craft of writing from many angles. Although potential authors dream of autograph parties, television appearances and Pulitzer Prizes, seldom do they understand what steps must be taken to achieve these heady aspirations.

To take this craft seriously, the student writer must first understand the power of the written word. The fact is: *Spoken words may change a single person or group of people. Written words carry the power to influence myriad generations and change the course of history.* If the craft is taken lightly, frivolous words written by rebels will degrade the languages of men and ultimately destroy the people. If, on the other hand, the student of words will use the keys to effective writing toward professionalism in this craft, he will indeed elevate the plateau of education and secure the foundation of his society.

This book takes the craft of writing from the creative viewpoint and opens the editorial door with *the secret keys* to understanding editorial needs and desires, the keys known and used by established professionals. Each step is carefully outlined and set in proper order. The keys are clearly stated and placed in the hands of the student. When these points are followed without reluctance and drops of perspiration drip from the writer's brow, then and only then will the student of writing wedge his foot in the editorial door and demand the undivided attention of the editor of his choice.

Thomas A. Noton
Author-Editor-Publisher

x

CONTENTS

PART ONE THE AUTHOR

That person (or persons) actually committing the concept to manuscript form.

CHAPTER ONE

Writing the Article

The unlearned author may desire to write for the slicks (magazines so named for their slick pages) because of the prestige or the money or both. Yet, in most cases, this novice writer's attempts will be returned with a form rejection slip signed by a non-editorial representative. These "mail openers" are hired by the editor to do just what their name implies. They open the mail looking for obvious rejects. They attach the form rejection slip and put the manuscript back into the mail before it even has a chance to cool from its trip across the country. (Mail openers are discussed in detail in Part II.)

The reasons these authors never get by the first desk are so common to editors that they give lists to new employees which detail the errors commonly committed by these novices.

The first reason for a manuscript's landing in the common rejection pile is found in the new writer's failure to understand the usual process of the entire publishing business. The novice feels that the writing is the only *real* concern in this business of words. Yet, the author has no part in the process of publishing if his work fails to meet the professional standard of the publishing house and its established audience. So, out of that understanding, the author can see that his part is not only to write exceptionally well, but he must be able to *slant* his material to a particular magazine's audience and deliver it in a *style* that the magazine's editor finds compelling.

Slant and style are necessary to the author of articles. Since each magazine is a composite of the personalities who put it together, that neatly stitched and trimmed mass of slick sheets has a personality of its own. That's easy to see when we take a look at two different publications. When comparing *Cosmopolitan* and *The Saturday Evening Post*, it's obvious that there is a vast difference in tone, content, slant, style and overall personality.

The difference begins in the philosophy of the leadership. Helen Gurley Brown at *Cosmopolitan* and Cory SerVaas at *The Saturday Evening Post* are diverse personalities; these personalities form the basis for the personalities of each of their publications. That difference is filtered down to the several management persons, and then on to the general staff. Ultimately, the tone of the cover reflects the personality of the magazine's content.

Even when magazines are aimed at the same basic audience, they still have personality traits that make them unique. So, a study of the markets and the individual magazines in those markets is the first purpose of the author who wishes to be consistently published. I've purposely added *consistently* to the previous sentence because an author may inadvertently hit on a sale or two without studying the markets.

UNDERSTANDING SLANT AND STYLE

The first key to becoming a successfully published author with a consistent track record and steady financial gain is found in the full understanding of *slant* and *style*.

The way many seasoned writers go about studying the markets, and the slants and styles of the various magazines in those markets is to visit the local library regularly. Since many individuals can't afford to subscribe to the wide range of magazines available that pay for freelance submissions, a trip to the library once or twice a week for a few hours of study can be an inexpensive way to hold an open file on hundreds of publications. Most of these magazines will furnish an author with writer's guidelines explaining their editorial slant and style upon request when supplied with a self-addressed, stamped envelope.

During a visit to the magazine section of the library, stop by the research (or resource) desk and ask the librarian for a few moments of her time. She is employed by the library to assist visitors with their needs, and will break away from her duties behind the desk and go through a tour of the magazine section with you. Some libraries set up the magazine section in alphabetical order, while others categorize the magazines according to their own system.

If you would like to see magazines not normally carried by your local library, it is not impossible to have your library borrow several back issues from another library.

Speaking of back issues: back issues are not out on the current issue racks, but are bound under a hard cover and displayed in another section of the library. The research librarian will help visitors find them in the *bound editions*.

As a young author, I was putting together an article about Georgia. I had some fine transparencies from a visit my wife and I had made through the state. We had interviewed some local people and had taken the grand tour through the archives. I had everything just right, and knew it was tailor-made for *National Geographic*. A letter to the editor told him of my article and the beautiful pictures that would accompany the extensive manuscript. When the editor wrote back and told me to check a certain back issue I was devastated. "We've recently done a spread on the beauty of Georgia," he wrote. I had failed to check the back issues, and consequently I was rejected.

A constant study of the individual publications is important as the first step toward publishing consistently.

FINE FINGER FOOD

Failing to keep abreast of current issues is a fault of many writers. We all live in a world of our own, and many times neglect to go beyond the four walls of our own lives. There's an old saying, "Us four and no more," that fits the personalities of too many writers today. The prevailing attitude appears to be that of an ostrich burying its head in the sand of his own desires instead of reaching out to a world that revolves around more than one man's ideas.

There is more to life than being a Democrat or a Republican, more than being black or white, anglo or hispanic. Life doesn't revolve around one single issue for the creative writer. The publishable writer reaches out beyond the scope of life he has experienced, and touches, grips and analyzes worlds far outside his own. He keeps in tune with what is happening in the lives of others and he finds current issues, fads, political views and social changes refreshing. He writes interesting stuff about those current ideas and situations.

I met a lady who broke into writing with an article titled, *"Fine Finger Food."* This lover of snacks suddenly realized that Nabisco and other major food producers were coming on fast with new products aimed at television viewers who like to munch while they watch. She began an extensive research program on what was happening in the field of snack food. She wrote to several of the companies who put new products on the market. Their replies brought her a shelf-full of finger food. She did some tests on granola bars, comparing one to another. (Some are hard and crunchy while others are soft and chewy.) This determined author also visited magazine racks in her local supermarket and the magazine section of her library to keep abreast of the food pages in the women's magazines. She noted that none of the major magazines were talking about the products and how they have come to have an effect on the American public, yet they were publishing articles all around the subject. She was elated. With notes to guide her, she wrote to the most likely editor (carefully noting the name and address of the food editor) and sent her a short, factual query. (Queries are covered in Part II.)

Within ten days she received a positive response and had her article in the mail before dusk. She carefully addressed the manuscript to the editor who had responded and also noted on the outside of the envelope that she was sending "Requested Material." She enclosed an SASE and sent it first class.

Now, a lesser writer would have sat back and anxiously waited for a response from this "big-time" publishing house. Her nails would have been bitten down to the quick and her hair slightly grayer from the passing of time. Not our girl. She moved right into more research on her subject, visiting the magazine section of the library once again. She hustled into the depths of the darker corners and searched out back issues of the publications that seemed promising. She was on hcr way to developing another article on her favorite subject: *food.*

CATCH A RISING STAR

I live in a medium-sized city in central Florida. Due to its proximity to the many attractions here, our city fathers decided to build a huge civic center with ample staging and seating for big-name performers. Some of the most exciting and best-known stars come to our city where they thrill tens of thousands with their shows. Out of this deep caldron of hype and show business a creative writer can draw a personality profile or an exclusive interview with a star.

Okay, so maybe you live in a small town and there is no civic center which attracts a cluster of stars sashaying across the stage, but you are probably within driving distance of a medium-sized city that does attract such personalities. You have a state fair, a county fair, country jamboree or some other function attracting performers. The creative writer or journalist will work at getting "in" with the producers of these shows, thus creating a line to the performer's manager and a possible exclusive personal interview with the star. The thinking writer will then solicit the use of a local professional photographer with a reputation of excellence and get him to tag along on the interview. Many local photographers will take dozens of pictures during the interview and provide the writer with some fine shots for his article. The photographer merely wants his name credited under each photo used. It's good promotion for him, and top-notch photos really add to the salability of an article. Poor photos or art work may ruin the effect of a good article, though, so be selective.

Editors are always looking for well-written celebrity interviews with excellent photos of the personality. Those familiar faces and names sell magazines, so they are always welcome.

AN HYPOTHESIS

So the producer puts the writer in touch with the manager of a big star who, in turn, sets up a special time and place for an interview. What then? What should the writer do to prepare for this once-in-a-lifetime opportunity? First, relax. Even though the "star" has exposure that makes him seem bigger than life, he is still a human being with the same problems, desires and feelings of inadequacy as each of the more than four billion other *homo sapiens* inhabiting this planet. So, relax and begin to outline the questions pertinent to his life. People are always happy to hear that a star's existence is similar to their own. It goes back to the reality of writing material with reader identification in mind. It is impossible to give you a standard format of questions to ask on each interview, but you are free to go to your library and search specific magazines and see (through the bound editions) which magazines run interviews on personalities similar to the one you have set up. Check the types of questions asked and make an outline with similar questions.

A FRAME OF REFERENCE

Your audience will want to know how the personality got to his present position of fame and financial success. The questions must be open-ended. Some famous people are really introverts who only come alive on stage. During an interview they may clam up, and you will have to pry them open with a creative approach. Provocative questions which cause a response beyond a simple "yes" or "no" will open the personality up and let the readers see what makes him tick. Good interview questions allow the reader to see what turns the star on and makes him move to higher ground, and what turns him off and causes him problems. These candid interviews sell magazines. So, direct questions that can be answered with short, simple answers must be avoided. The best way to begin sentences which will elicit an extensive response are typically, "Tell us how you . . ." or "Would you explain why you began your . . ." or "What would you say are the steps toward . . ." With beginnings like these, the person being interviewed must seriously consider your question and formulate an extensive answer.

If the personality has a special trait, hobby, love situation or some other characteristic which gives the opportunity for insight, the astute writer/interviewer will home in on that aspect and pull out interesting and unknown sidelights about him.

A short interview with the star's manager (or the person who actually set up the interview) will be of value. Ask him what turns on the star and what areas to avoid. He'll gladly tell you, because he wants the interview to go well too. It's good publicity. Extensive research prior to the actual interview will create a more relaxed atmosphere. The interviewer will feel comfortable knowing he has a satchelfull of information, and the personality will be flattered that the author took the time to research. When both parties are relaxed, the interview becomes conversational instead of bound by that restrictive feeling found in some interviews. The flow is easy and gives the reader a feeling of being there.

Once the interview is complete, and assuming it went well and the person interviewed is indeed a star, now what? Well, it's back to the library and back to studying *slant* and *style*. Check the back issues of those magazines likely to use material about personalities similar to the one you've interviewed. Now that you have had the talk with the star, you will be better able to select a likely editor for your piece. Be certain you go back to those bound editions and study several issues to be certain the magazine of your choice hasn't already run something on your man. After a decision is made, a short, well-written query to the magazine's editor will either result in an open door or give you a quick indication that he is not interested in your interview. If the latter occurs, simply go to your second choice from the magazine rack and query that editor. If that doesn't bring a positive response, go to your third choice. If that doesn't do it, then . . . well, you've got the picture. This is a *never give up* business.

CONTROVERSIAL ISSUES

Some magazines thrive on controversial issues. "Hot items" are always in demand by editors of weekly magazines and some monthly periodicals. If your subject is something that's "in the news" and you have a handle on the issue, by all means look for the magazine whose slant and style can be followed and get the job done.

There are those times when a phone call to the editor of a magazine will be received with a positive response. Those instances are extremely rare. But, if you have a piece with special photos that would fit a magazine's slant and you know its deadline, and you just can't possibly wait for the overnight delivery service, then try a call. Otherwise, send it through the post office.

Controversial issues must have a strong *reader hook*, yet the hook must not reveal the author's stand on the subject. If the hook gives away too much slant on the subject, the reader will know the gist of the article before he begins it and therefore has no need to read it through.

THE TRIED AND TRUE

Even if you can't find any controversial issues around your town and nobody of "star" quality ever comes within a hundred miles and your interest doesn't lie in current issues, you have an alternative.

You can write about what you know and live with every day. *Reader's Digest* (maybe you've heard of that magazine) has published stories about unforgettable people for years. *Grit* brings homespun profiles of people and places with every issue. Maybe there's a special pond near your town where you can find the solitude lacking in so many urban lives today, and you can describe it so well that the reader will drop his briefcase in the middle of his active schedule just to bathe himself in the scenery your words have painted. The pungent odor of pine and new-mown meadows fill his nostrils, bring back many of his boyhood wonders. Your words cause him to squint at the bright rays bouncing off the glassy surface of that old pond as a bullfrog belches out his foghorn call against the stillness of the midsummer day. The reader can smell the lilies of spring, or see the golden leaves of fall as Indian summer brings on a dazzling array of colors. You may bring a shiver to the reader as you create a chilly winter draft, or describe ice fishing on a frozen river.

Creating the desire to "get away from it all just for a day" is good reading to the busy executive, the overworked secretary or the harried homemaker.

PEOPLE WATCHERS

In general, people are people watchers. We all like to see what the next guy is up to. We learn from watching. We laugh. We sympathize and we emphathize. As we linger and look, time is suspended as we take it all in. There's the old couple who seem more in love than a couple of teenagers. Their bony hands reach out to one another as they walk along the busy street. They've been together so long that they've begun to look alike. Our scrutinization doesn't change anything, but we smile and think of how we will be when we grow older. There is a moment of wonder and reflection as we watch others.

People magazine is proof enough that we all like to read about people. Sure, famous people are more easily pushed onto covers of such magazines, but those of us who are lesser known (somewhere deep in the magazine's pages) are fun to read about too. It's always great to read about some individual or group of people who are what we tag "characters." They give us a chuckle because they seem to have all the same thoughts and desires as the rest of us, yet these people have the guts to express themselves openly while we sit back and keep our mouths shut. In many cases those "characters" interest the general audiences because the audience vicariously lives that life through reading about them. So, the *character sketch* article has a place in the American magazine industry.

The following character sketch has been taken from one of my previous books, *The Joy of Writing.* Although this character is not a real person, he could have been. In fact, he might be a composite of several characters I've met.

Uncle Vester's Private War

The "Yankee money grabbers in their fine machines," was what Uncle Vester called passers-by roaring past the front of his mountain home like Offenhausers at Indianapolis. He vented his animosity for them with every name he could come up with. His tobacco-stained, white beard flapped up and down as he mumbled about the polluted air, the noise of the speeding cars and the "smart-alecky Yankees."

The split-log cabin sat so close to the main highway that gusts from the Mack trucks would make the old place quiver. There were times when Uncle Vester told me, "Them dadburn buggies is comin' through the front door." He had had quite a hassle with state and federal authorities about his right to remain in the place when the big road was built. Uncle Vester won — or had he?

Whenever I sat with the old gentleman, he would rock for silent hours. Then without warning, he would get up, go into the shaky mountain home and bring out his nine-stringed banjo, plop back down in the rocker and finger the strings. He would slap his knee with a howl and let his fingers slide across the frets like lightning. Fast picking and loud singing rang through the mountains, bouncing back in harmony. Tourists slowed their pace to hear more. Uncle Vester would strum and yodel until several cars had pulled to the side of the road and stopped. People would get out of their automobiles and lean on the white picket fence just ten or twelve feet from the front porch. His rocking and picking, and singing at the top of his lungs, were something to experience. All of a sudden though, Uncle Vester would stop, jump up, start toward the door, look back at all the smiling faces, spit, turn on his heels and go inside mumbling, "Them stupid gawkin' touristers!"

Sometimes when the old man was in the mood, he would run his hands down the legs of his bib-overalls, as if that simple act could clean his calloused palms, and then he would say, "Well, Sonny, let's say we eat a little sumthin'."

My name isn't Sonny, but Uncle Vester didn't like "the ring a' that Yankee name, William."

He would disappear into the old-fashioned kitchen,

stopping at the door long enough to chide, "We havin' Yankee pot roast," then roar with laughter.

After I seated myself at the dining table, Uncle Vester would bring out a steaming bowl of hog jowls and black-eyed peas, a platter heaped with cornbread and dripping with fresh-churned butter. The aroma made my mouth water.

With fork poised, I would dig in, and the old mountaineer would say, "Hold on, Sonny. We ain't told the Lord we thankful fer it yet."

He took off his weather-worn straw hat and lay it next to the cornbread, folded his knotty hands and closed his twinkling blue eyes. "Lord, we sure are thankful for the food ya put on this here table, and we ain't forgettin' the good health ya give us neither. Dear Lord, I-I do want to ast ya one thing. Would you have them move their road somewheres else, so's a body can get a good night's sleep? Thank you for list'nin'. Amen." He pulled out his big red handkerchief and blew, foghorn style. "Dig in, Sonny! Ya ain't gonna grow less' ya eat!"

One evening in late June after an especially sumptuous meal by mountain standards, we rested on Uncle Vester's porch, watching the Tennessee sun slip quietly behind the mountain slopes. The swish of passing cars was diminishing, and the air smelled sweet and fresh. We sat rocking and talking about his boyhood days. He told me of the Civil War in which his granddaddy had fought so bravely.

Although he had told it many times, tears still filled his eyes as he recounted the news of death at Wilson's Creek, July 21, 1861, of his mother's weeping, and his own vow to "git even with them Yanks." He reassured me he had broken that vow. In fact, Uncle Vester made quite an issue of the fact that he really "loved 'em."

Reminiscing made us oblivious of time, and the mountains began to cast their dark shadows across the highway in front of the shack. The lights of passing cars shared the scene with us.

Late into the evening one of the cars flashed its lights on the porch and came to a sudden stop. The typical tourist poked his head out of the window and yelled, "Hey, Joe, do you know where I turn to get to Memphis?"

Uncle Vester rose slowly. His eyes gained a certain twinkle, and his mouth struggled with a slight smile. "How'd ya know my name was Joe, mister?" Uncle Vester drawled.

The driver was delighted. "Hey, I just guessed," he laughed, eyebrows raised.

"If'n yer so good at guessin'," the old man said, "then ya kin guess where ya turn to get to Memphis!" With that, he whirled on one heel and went into the cabin, his beard flapping as he mumbled, "Stupid Yankees."

18- THE EDITORIAL DOOR

CHAPTER TWO

Writing the Short Story

The short story is just what it says it is: *short*. The average short story is under 5,000 words. Usually the article and the short story run in the 3,000-word range. The short, short story, about 800 to 1500 words, and the novelette, up to 15,000 words, are mutations of the short story.

Since the story is short, there is less room to maneuver and therefore it is much tougher to write. Yet many novice writers attempt to begin their careers with the short story. The prevailing idea is that short means simple and simple means easy. It appears to be the easiest way to become a published author. Wrong! Writing a short story probably affords the new author the least possibility of publication. First, about one-tenth of published works in the 3,000-word range are short stories. The bulk of material in most magazines is made up of articles, not short stories. That alone puts the squeeze on the new author. Coupled with it is the fact that the short story must be written with a great economy of words, something not usually inherent in the novice writer. Frugality with words is an art that is learned the hard way: by experience. It is perfected by plenty of editing and rewriting. The author becomes so familiar with his thesaurus and dictionary that he begins to "feel" whether he has used the correct word or not.

During my seminars, I write an exercise on the chalkboard. It goes like this:

The happy couple danced and skipped through the cornfield, laughing hilariously as they whirled among the stalks.

I then ask the class to edit the sentence, attempting to use the greatest economy of words. I challenge them to attempt to use half the words and still maintain the original visual effect.

After everyone has worked on the project for a few minutes, I ask several to read what they've written. Some are very good, while others fail to maintain the original scene or edit judiciously. But there always seems to be one student who catches that "just right" word and rewrites the sentence like this.

The happy couple *frolicked* among the cornstalks.

So (with just under half the words) that single sentence has given the same visual effect with a greater economy of words. The word *frolicked* brings the entire intent of the other words, *danced, skipped, laughing* and *whirled*, into focus.

It is with this frugality of words that the short story writer brings his characters to life, paints his scenery and builds a strong plot. Brevity is essential, so the writer must learn to use the tools of his trade with exactness. Each word must be well thought out and placed in conjunction with the words around it to give the reader a concise understanding of all the author is trying to convey.

THE STORY

Now that we understand what short is, let's take a look at what a story is and how it comes into being.

The phase, "Once upon a time," begins many stories for children. That four-word opening gives the idea that the tale is fantasy and therefore *time* and *place* are irrelevant. It doesn't matter if the story is set in New York around the turn of the century, or in Elba, Alabama, in the mid-fifties. It can be any place and any time. The story continues: " . . . there were three little pigs." Well, now we have the protagonists. These lead characters are introduced right away. That's good writing. The reader wants to get to know the lead character (or characters) in the story so he can have a vicarious experience. Reader identification is very important, and the more quickly the lead character is introduced the more the reader learns about him and identifies with him. Let's go on with the breakdown of this fascinating story. What we see next is simply a *problem*. The three guys break up and go their separate ways. The question before each of them is where to live safely. So, the first protagonist decides to build his house out of straw. He does so and the problem worsens. Not only does he lose his abode, but he also has to flee for his life from a ravenous wolf (the antagonist in this story). The conflict deepens as the first little pig is hot-footin' it to the second pig's home, which is made of sticks. The hungry wolf is already huffing and puffing due to the cross-country chase to catch that greased pig, but when he gets to the stick house, he promises to get his second wind and blow the house down. Sure enough, he succeeds and the problem grows deeper. Now these two squeakers head to big brother's house of bricks, scoot inside and slam the door in the wolf's face.

Let's take a look at what has taken place so far. (We don't want to take too much time on this synopsis because we want to get back to the story and find out what happens next.) Well, up to this point, we have seen two of the three protagonists nearly lose their lives. Their homes were destroyed and they are being pursued by a villainous enemy. The problem began quickly in this story and hasn't let up one bit. In fact, it has been getting worse by the minute. Now, through strong reader identification, we are standing in the living room of that third pig's mansion and we're shivering with fright with those three little oinkers. Our palms are wet and the hair on the backs of our necks is standing on end.

Back to the story: The swooshing wind of wolf's breath is whistling around the corners of the brick structure, but nothing is moving. The house is secure and the piggies are safe. In fact, we're all saved from that fearsome grouch who wants to gobble us up. Just to make certain, though, the oldest pig takes a look out of the window. "Oh no!" he screams. "We've piled all this furniture up against the door and we can't get out."

The other two look at him. One smirks, "Why would we want to get out? Wolf's out there."

The older pig rolls his eyes in disgust. "I know that," he grumbles. "But I thought you'd like to know he's trying to get up on the roof so he can come down the chimney to gobble us up."

With that declaration, the pigs frantically dash every which way squeaking their heads off. It seems that in spite of everything they've tried to do to keep the enemy away and save themselves from disaster, all is lost. They have come to that indisputable corner and they are trapped and will fall prey to that carnivorous beast.

Wait! There is one last chance for them to save themselves. The biggest bacon says, "Let's build a fire and boil some water. When he finally does get up on the roof and come down the chimney, he'll fall into the water and that will cook his goose." So that's what the three pigs did, and the story had a happy and satisfying ending with the problem solved. The major conflict was over and the readers felt a sense of victory.

This simple children's tale really has all the elements of good story writing. It has a protagonist (three of them) identifiable to the audience to which the story is aimed. It has a problem that, within the realm of fantasy in children's stories, is feasible. The problem worsens and finally comes to a point where all seems lost. Then, through the efforts of the protagonists, a logical (again, within the realm of children's fantasy) solution is formulated and pulled off in time to save their porkskins and give the reader a satisfying solution.

So, now we can define a story in a few simple words.

A story is an interesting combination of words which produce a problem; a deepening of that problem; a point at which that problem seems insurmountable; and a final solution of that problem to the complete satisfaction of the reader.

This is a simplified definition, but it is easy to see that all stories follow this some line — and the story doesn't have to be fictional. Let's take a look at a few examples of the writings that fall into this definition.

The well-known book, *How To Win Friends and Influence People* by Dale Carnegie, is a good book to take a look at to see if it fits. First, Mr. Carnegie's book begins with an understood protagonist: *the reader.* The problem is introduced as something understood. The reader is having problems socially and wishes to overcome this obstacle keeping him from enjoying the company of others and allowing others to enjoy his company. The solution is graphically given and is progressive from chapter to chapter. By the time the reader has completed the book, he should have the solution and be satisfied that the problem is overcome in his life.

Since we've covered nursery rhymes and a book on winning friends, let's take this idea to the ultimate. Let's see if this definition of a story fits the Book of Books, the Bible. *Time* and *place* are set right away. The book begins by orienting the reader. The protagonist is mankind and the forces of evil provide the antagonist. A problem is produced (in the Garden of Eden) that gets worse as mankind continues on its course. All appears to be lost until a Savior is provided in the New Testament and the solution to man's problem brings satisfaction to the reader.

I wrote the book, *Thieves*. Let's see if this novel fits the pattern I've set for a story. It's the story of a young man who is part of a band of thieves. He falls in love and determines to leave the band and get a decent job, then marry his love and live happily ever after. The band leader threatens him with the death of his sweetheart unless he submits to one last big heist. The problem deepens and the drama and action merge to create tension as the point of insurmountability dawns on the reader. Finally, the solution brings about a satisfying ending and the book is closed with the reader wearing a smile.

All stories don't have to be in book form, nor do they have to be in short story form. Many articles fit the definition of a story. I wrote an article for *Writer's Digest* (Feb. '82) about the craft of writing for the inspirational market. I noted the protagonist as the person who wanted to write, yet had no training in the craft. The *problem* was getting published. The more that writer wrote, the worse things got. I then proceeded to give the would-be writer tips on how to create salable material. Thus, we had the problem and the solution and all the stuff in between.

THE READER HOOK

Beginning properly is the most important part of writing. If the writer fails to hook the reader's attention, the reader loses interest and the story goes unread. Good beginnings are packed with dramatic words, and yet they give the reader a complete sense of *when* and *where* the scene is taking place.

I'll solidify what I'm saying with an example of an opening I used in an article on religious writing. I titled it, *"Inspired Writing: A Fallacy"*. Here are the opening lines:

> A man caught me in the foyer of our church. His wife stood at his side. Both of them displayed a Cheshire cat smirk as he flatly stated, "I sent a manuscript off to the same company that published your first book." The sound of it rang in my ears with that *na-na-na-na-na-na* of the bully on my block when I was a kid.
>
> Childhood recall made me want to scream, "I'm gonna tell my mother on you." Instead, I tried to be kind. "Oh," I said. I smiled. "You've written a book?" I knew the man and knew he had no training as a writer. He appeared to me to think himself above such trivial matters.
>
> His wife began to smile and nod her head enthusiastically as he responded. "I was praying one day last week and suddenly God began to give me the words for a teaching book." As he paused for impact, I swallowed, dreading what I was in for. He continued, "I mean it. The words came to me so fast that I could hardly keep up with all God was giving me." He snorted and shook his head. "I'm telling you, this book is directly from God's own mouth."

From this opening, *time* and *place* are established quickly and real people are introduced immediately. Although this is an article and not a fictional story, the same principles have been applied to hook the reader's attention and pull him into the "story." The reader is completely oriented and can follow the action, dialogue and line of thinking easily.

One of the major faults of novice writers is the idea that good writing should present a mystery for the reader and thus lure him into reading on to find out what on earth is happening. That false impression seems to run rampant among beginning writers. The novice must realize that a vague opening only serves to mystify the reader and leave him cold. The reader wants to (must) understand what's going on and where he is. Note: I used the phrase, *where he is*. The reader must actually feel he is a part of what is going on and *that he's in the scene.* If he doesn't have that sense, then he understands he is only reading a story and that does not fulfill his need to escape. Now, I'm not just talking about fiction, either. The first-person stories found in such periodicals as *Reader's Digest* must carry these same elements. And it's easy to see that articles such as the opening of the one I wrote for religious writers must also create such strong reader identification that the reader is immersed in the reading.

Although the story a writer is telling may be about an actual person's life, it need not be burdened with the restrictions of that life. Mixing fact with a touch of fiction for flavor is a common practice.

Here's an example of an opening scene which may be factual or fictional:

A Pit of Darkness

The wail of a siren was barely audible above the thunderous pounding of the surf. A midnight rain pelted the deserted beach at Key West as a disheveled man struggled out of the water. He squinted up the beach toward the glow of bright lights and the sound of heavy metal rock music. He felt tired and dizzy, and he staggered. Everything lost its perspective. He crumpled to the wet sand.

The tide was rising and the surf washed up to lick his bare feet and touch the ragged hem of his pants. His breathing was barely perceptible, yet he was alive; and despite overexposure for more days than he could remember, he was stable. He lay there unable to move away from the water's edge.

The sound of the siren faded into the night and the pounding of drums and clashing of cymbals gave way to the rumbling surf. The waves nearly drowned out the gasping breaths of two teenaged boys as they sprinted over the sticky sand. They whispered secretively as they darted past an old bench and down toward the water. One of the boys clutched a chrome-plated revolver. He held it high and grinned triumphantly. "Now we can get anything we want," he boasted. Suddenly the other boy grabbed his companion's arm and pulled him to a stop. The clouds parted and they could see the man lying in a crumpled heap on the packed sand. The revolver glistened in the moonlight.

THE DISSECTION

Let's take a look at this opening.

First, does it sound like it could be factual as well as fictional? Does it open with a reader hook? In other words, do you want to know what happens next? Has a basic time and place been given? Can the reader follow the storyline and action?

The answers are all *yes*.

To add to the intrigue of this opening, a siren was used. Any time a siren wails in the night, interest is enhanced. So, the hook is integrated into the first paragraph along with time and place. What the author must do is stop after he's written his opening and ask a few simple questions:

Where am I?
On a beach in Key West.
What time is it?
Midnight.
Are there any conditions of interest?
Light rain. Distant sound of rock music. Mysterious person. Two boys with a revolver.
Is the reader hooked?
Yes. The reader will want to know *who, what, how* and *why* about this man who has emerged from the surf. The reader will also want to know what these two boys will do with the revolver and what relationship they will have with the stranger crumpled on the sand.

CONTEMPORARY SUBJECTS

The power to *convey, transform* and *encourage* is at the disposal of the writer. A responsibility comes with that power, and the writer must face life and contemporary issues with a broad field of vision and a depth of insight. Stories of people who have overcome obstacles that seemed beyond their capabilities, or profiles of the famous, the rich, the "characters" who are found seated on the park benches across the nation are all lively possibilities for contemporary writing.

I read the true story of a famous detective who has no hands. He has hooks that work mechanically, secret pistols stuck up his sleeves, armor-plated automobiles, airplanes, and hidden devices on his body. The story of this man's life was intriguing and the opening reader hook excited me. Does this article/story really fit the definition of a story? Sure it does. It's the story of a man (protagonist) who has a problem (no hands) and the problem is brought to a solution (the use of gadgets) that completely satisfies the reader.

Another contemporary article/story one might think couldn't fit our story definition would be an article about a fashion model. Let's see if we can make it work.

The article begins with the idea that modeling is a glamorous business with popping flashbulbs and the opportunity to "make it big" in Hollywood. Any time glamour, money or prestige is the subject, people are interested. The *subject* becomes the reader hook.

As the article unfolds, a single model is profiled to produce the protagonist. The article candidly looks at the "real life" of a model — her struggles to overcome what she has discovered to be less than glamorous circumstances: the photographer's couch, the need to remain thin, the erratic work schedule and the fact that only the top models make a lot of money in the business. Yet, with all these problems, this young model has found her niche and is completely fulfilled. The solution to the problems was her ability to cope with each one in turn and maintain her desire to succeed. So, in this case, coping is a solution in itself.

Readers need to have a "they lived happily ever after" ending in order to experience real satisfaction. Since the writer has given the reader a vicarious experience with the protagonist, whatever the protagonist experiences, the reader will experience. Satisfaction for one is satisfaction for the other.

Unfortunately, a short while back it became popular

to write stories that "gave life as it really is — cruel." These stories left the reader unfulfilled. Yes, we do have to face life every day. Yes, we do have a cruel existence at times. That's all the more reason to understand that our readers want to read about those who have gotten a victory in their lives. Because of our desire to be winners, we automatically attach ourselves to winners. That's done, in part, by reading about winners. Movie stars, television personalities, the rich, the famous are all perceived as winners, so the general public identifies with them through the many articles written about them.

So remember, whether it's fiction or fact, the same definition of a story applies.

32- THE EDITORIAL DOOR

.

CHAPTER THREE

Writing the Book

The major difference between writing a book and writing an article or short story is simply the length of the work. But there *are* other factors that come into play because of the manuscript's length.

Certainly the research must be more extensive and it takes longer to write, but beyond that there is a psychological factor. A book seems like an awful lot of work. Why write a book when a shorter piece will do? The idea of beginning with 200 blank sheets of paper and filling them with something worthy of people's sitting down and taking their valuable time to read is beyond many writers' comprehension. Look at the

180 pages left to write after you've spilled your heart on 20 pages (which a new writer views as quite an effort in itself). The work you put into these pages could have made a short story or an article, and the thing would be over with and sealed and on its way to an editor. But instead, you still have 280 blank sheets of white paper to deal with. What a drag.

Knowing all this, the new author sets out to write his masterpiece. Whether he is writing a nonfiction book on the latest craze or putting together a novel, he must face the fact that research is necessary. Just as a writer must research any of his works, he must do the same with longer pieces. The research of my novel, *Thieves*, took a full four months of intensive study and note taking. I used the library, books I owned, information gathered from friends and associates and clippings from newspapers and magazines. Of all the sources at my disposal, my research librarian proved to be the key to gathering the details I needed to give my novel the professional appeal and little-known facts that added a special touch to its theme.

THE OUTLINE

After the research is complete and all the facts are gathered, it is absolutely necessary to put them in order. The novice writer shrugs his shoulders and says, "I thought I was going to write, not dig for details and make outlines. If I wanted to be a file clerk, I would have joined an office staff." Professional writing is a combination of all the aspects of proper preparation. Digging for details and putting them in proper order is a major part of the writing life. Writing — that is, actually putting words on paper in manuscript form — is only part of what a writer does to make his work look as though it flowed from his fertile imagination without effort. The real pro works harder than anyone else to make it look easy, while those who don't know how tough it is stand back in admiration. They are awed by the "talented, gifted, wondrous" thing he's accomplished. They say, "If only God had given me that gift."

When the writer understands the work involved in writing and pushes himself beyond the others, those who quit when the going gets rough wonder how he did it and declare him *gifted*.

Now, let's go to work.

THE ACTUAL OUTLINE

The outline always begins with an understanding of direction. Where will the writing go? That understanding is accomplished through the use of a synopsis. It may be a simple sentence or two, or it may be a paragraph or a page, but it must be just what the name implies: a general view of the overall manuscript in a brief statement.

After that general statement is made comes the actual outline structuring.

Remember the formal outline your English professor followed the same way your English teacher did in junior high school? First there was the Roman numeral that indicated the first major point. Then, an upper case letter (A., B., C., D., etc.) gave the succession of minor points which dealt with that major point. Under those upper case English letters, Arabic numerals listed the subpoints, and if the listing called for sub-subpoints, then the lower case English lettering system followed.

Yeech! That's as bad as having to diagram a sentence isn't it? Well, believe it or not, your English teacher won't be looking over your shoulder as a freelance writer and you won't have to go in to all that detail. But I suggest you do use a system of some kind. If you don't, you won't be able to understand your own outline. I use upper case letters for my major points and numbers underneath for my minor points. I then attempt to list them in the order of their importance. After I've completed that, I go back over the outline, editing and revising it until everything's in the proper order.

Remember, the outline is not for your exclusive use. The outline, a synopsis and three sample chapters may be what an editor requests after you query him. That's a common thing today and your outline had better be a readable, understandable piece of writing. If your outline is written in some code only you understand, the editor will surely think your manuscript must be as unintelligible and send the whole thing back with a little note telling you to forget about a career in writing.

THE ACTUAL WRITING

So, the research is complete and the synopsis and outline are finished too. It's time to write.

The actual manuscript must, first of all, look professional. In order to have a positive reading from an editor, the manuscript must be neat and clean and possess the characteristics of a professionally written piece. So make certain the keys on your typewriter are clean and free from clogs in the o's or e's, which detract from the crisp copy necessary for a professional look. Always use white paper, 8½" by 11" sheets only. A good grade of white paper (20-pound bond is best) should be used for the final draft of the manuscript. Many modern copy machines will copy on any type or grade of paper, so even copies may be reproduced on a good grade of bond paper. Single spacing may be used on the query to the editor, but never use single spacing on the actual manuscript. If a cover letter is used, it may be single-spaced, but the actual manuscript must be double-spaced. Leave a 1"-1½" margin all around. That leaves room for editor's notations to the typesetter and printer.

To begin the first sheet, put your name and complete address in the upper left corner in single-spaced lines about an inch from the left and an inch from the top. You may wish to put your phone number and / or social security number under your address. Tell the editor what rights you are selling. If you've done your market research (whether for a magazine or a book publisher) you already know what rights they *usually* buy. After you've put your personal information in the upper left corner, roll the sheet down so that the top of the sheet and the bottom of the sheet meet above the roller. You will then be typing just above the middle of the page. That's a great place to center your title. After the title is typed in the center of the page, double-space and center your byline. The use of pseudonyms is old-fashioned, so use your own name. Your title and byline should look something like this:

Getting Your Foot in the Editorial Door

By Thomas A. Noton

If you are writing a book, you'll want to double-space again and center the words, *Chapter One*, and, if it is nonfiction, the title of the first chapter under that. If it is fiction, you may dispense with the chapter title. (Modern fiction doesn't usually have chapter titles.)

So, in all, it will look like this:

Getting Your Foot in the Editorial Door

By Thomas A. Noton

Chapter One

Writing The Article

Now that you have all the preliminary stuff on the sheet in proper order, the editor has found out who you are, where you live, the title of your work and all the other little goodies he needs to know. Now skip four lines, indent five spaces and start typing the body of your manuscript. You are now writing in a professional manner. Your stuff looks good and you feel good about it.

THE GENERAL INTEREST BOOK

All manuscripts must begin with the professional format shown above. The content of the book (as with the article or short story) must grab the reader's attention and make him want to read on. So we're back to reader hook. The opening hook in long manuscripts may be more than a single sentence or paragraph. It may take several paragraphs in a succession of linking parts to make up the whole reader hook. An example is this intriguing beginning to Dr. Dennis Hensley's self-help book on success and prosperity,

Positive Workaholism (R & R Newkirk, Indianapolis, IN, 1983, used by permission.)

Chapter One

An Art of Work

For several years I worked as editor-in-chief of a magazine which was published for graduates of a small college in the Midwest. From time to time my editorial board and I would poll our readers to discover what they liked best about our publication — our front page articles? our feature stories? the photographs we ran? our sports reports? our ads?

The results of these surveys always came back to us with the same opening response, phrased in one form or another: "My favorite section of your magazine is the last page, where the alumni news is printed."

I've talked with dozens of other editors of college magazines and they've told me their surveys elicit the same response. And do you know why this is? It's because people want to see what their old friends have done in life so that they can compare how they stack up against them.

If you are in the habit of reading college alumni news notes, or if you've ever picked up one of those "Where Are They Now" booklets at your high school class reunions, you've probably already discovered something interesting. Although everyone listed had a similar beginning (same age, same graduation year, same teachers, etc.), no two wound up with identical lives, much less identical accomplishments.

Or the two boys who were co-captains of the football

team, there is one who now is a U.S. senator and the other who is a barber. Of the two girls who graduated at the head of the class, there is one who now is a movie star and the other who is a part-time crossing guard. Of your two closest chums, there is one who now is a vice president of a computer company and the other who is a piano tuner.

Why the vast differences in outcomes? Why the tremendous variation in success levels? Why the amazing ranges in personal advancement?

Sure, all of your friends are working and supporting themselves and are even serving society in useful occupations. But why is it that some of them have been able to gain wealth, fame and power while the others have had to settle for routine jobs and run-of-the-mill lives?

The answer is this: *Each person had a different attitude toward work, and it was this attitude that shaped his or her destiny.*

AN ANALOGY

Why does Dr. Hensley's book get the reader's attention? He used one of the most basic reader hooks. It's called the *relation hook*. The reader can *relate* to what is being said. In this case, he begins with college alumni and the inquisitiveness we've all felt at times. Most readers can relate to that from high school (as Dr. Hensley points out) so even if the reader never went to college he can still relate to what's been written. The reader is hooked. Dr. Hensley deepens the hook with another hook of like kind. First he appeals to the *inquisitiveness* of the human spirit, then he relates to man's *determination to succeed*. Hensley gives the reader the feeling that he is going to uncover secrets never understood by modern man, secrets that will give the reader a pathway to money, fame and power. (At least there seems to be an underlying innuendo to that effect.)

So, *Positive Workaholism*, a book for the general audience, has created a fine reader hook through the use of reader identification.

After the hook has been set, the writer must carry the reader into his book with crisp writing. Information which is either little known, or is well known but has a new slant, must fill the pages following the hook.

Too many writers hook the reader's attention for the first chapter and then drop the literary ball, leaving the reader with the feeling he has been cheated. He purchased the book based on the good writing found in the first chapter. But after he got to chapter three he discovered that chapter one was a fluke, chapter two died a slow death, and chapter three never did have life. He skipped to chapter six in hopes of finding vitality. When it wasn't there, he slammed the book on his desk and grumbled about paying good money for nothing but junk.

One thing is certain. That reader will note the name of the author and the publishing company. He may even write to the publisher and complain about that author, his book and the editorial staff who allowed such a book to be published. Just a few of those complaints will elicit a memo from the publisher to the editor: "The above-named author is not to be published by this company in the future."

So, strong writing must follow your hook. That strong writing is accomplished through study and practice. Proper research must have taken place prior to your first writing on the subject. For Dr. Hensley, the research was done through his experiences, as well as researching other books of like kind, magazine articles and business reports. Hensley has lived the successful life of the master accomplisher. Yet, even with all that going for him, Dennis Hensley had to read and interview and check with others who understood his subject. He had to take notes, make a synopsis of his book, write an outline and begin the work.

The writing life is not an easy one. Certainly there are autograph parties and television interviews. Yes, the best-selling authors get big bucks. It's true, a novelist who signs a movie contract may never have to work at another thing as long as he lives, but that doesn't keep him from having to struggle, research, outline and actually write in his lonely room while producing that big, smash best-seller. If he is truly a writer, he will continue to write, even after he has hit the big-time. That writing will take as much research as ever, as much struggle, as much outlining and as much lonely writing as it ever did. *Each manuscript must stand on its own merit.* Sure, it's easier to get a foot in the editorial door after you've had a hit, but that doesn't mean the author who has that hit can afford to produce sloppy work.

WRITING THE NOVEL

A novel is a long short story. How's that for simplicity?

People read for two basic reasons: *information* (such as that given in Dr. Hensley's book) or *escape* (found in fictional stories for the most part).

The novel is a fictional work designed to give the reader a lengthy escape from the rigors of daily living. Therefore, the definition of a story found in the previous chapter encompasses the novel as well as the short story, article, biography and other book forms.

Since the reader wishes to escape, *reader identification* is extremely important. If the reader cannot identify with the lead character in the book, he cannot escape into the story with the lead character. When the author does his job and writes with clarity, projecting the characters as alive, flesh-and-blood beings, then the reader will identify with the story, the problem and ultimately with the solution.

The vast difference between writing the short story and the novel is simply economy. Not that the author has words to waste in writing the novel, but he does have more room to expand the scenes, bring the characters to life and add touches from the five senses. In the shorter work he must dispense with much of that "flavor" and get down to the plot (problem and solution), using only those words which will move the story to its conclusion.

I'm not implying that writing a novel is easier than writing a shorter work. Although in some areas it seems to be so, in the overall picture, the work is still the work and it must be done well in order to be worthy of publication.

As the author, you must begin to *live* your book. As mentioned, Dr. Dennis Hensley lived his book before he wrote it. He considers himself a positive workaholic, so he has drawn from his experiences. The novelist must also draw from his experiences. He must relive those portions of his book which come from his own past. To give an example, I drew on my youth in Detroit to recall the thinking of a thief when I wrote my novel, *Thieves*. The gathering of gang members, the planning of a theft, the arguing and fighting among the members of the gang, and the total repugnance for any form of law or authority all stemmed from the life I'd lived. My former gambling habit, my foul language, my ill-will toward those who opposed my views — all of it come from the way I lived as a youth on the streets. Because I *lived* the story, my readers attest, "I began reading and couldn't put it down. It was as though I had entered into the pages of that book and begun to *live* it."

Although *Thieves* is a period book, and many of these line the shelves of libraries across the nation, the trend today is toward contemporary fiction.

Contemporary fiction dwells on the story line rather than the setting, the dress, the language or the give-and-take of the hero and heroine. The story line must be simple for the modern romances, yet it can be very complex for the general audience novel.

Since this book is an overview of creative writing, the specifics of putting your book on paper are not covered. (I've given a detailed teaching on writing in my previous book, *The Joy of Writing.*) There are many other books on the market covering the specific aspects of this craft.

In spite of this, we must become a bit more myopic in our view of what it takes to get the job done. If we back off and try to view the craft from a distance, we will lose perspective. The following chapter gives us a close look at certain facets.

CHAPTER FOUR

Once Upon a Time . . .

A student of writing (as opposed to a writer) caught me in the hall after class one day. He had been under my teaching periodically for about two years. He had heard my complete course, taken notes, attempted to do his best on the written tests and now stood before me with a wrinkled brow and pursed lips. "I want to write," he mumbled, "but getting all those words on the paper is a fearful thing." He looked at me with sad eyes. "I know what I want to write, but I don't think I have enough words to fill that many sheets of paper." He gave a nervous laugh. "I don't know how to fill in or even how to begin."

By then I was upset. Here this guy was, some twenty-one or twenty-two years old, who'd sat under my teaching for weeks at a time telling me he didn't learn how to begin. Not only that, he wanted to "fill in" the spaces to make the thing long enough for a book. (As though "fill-in" words would create a salable work). I took a deep breath and considered my own plight when I was in college. I looked at him and took another breath. "So, what do you want to write?" I asked.

"I would like to write a novel."

"A novel?"

"Sure."

"You know what this novel is going to be about?"

"I have the basic plot in my head."

"Why isn't it on paper?"

He just looked at me and swallowed. I could tell he was afraid to put it on paper, because it might be seen by someone who would laugh or reject it in some other way. "I can't," he replied.

"Can't?" I said. "I don't understand that word."

"I don't know how to begin."

I leaned against the rough wall of the hallway and sighed. "You must begin all stories with a concept. In order to understand your concept, you must write down a story to yourself, telling yourself what your story is going to be. That way, the story formulates in your mind while you are putting it on paper." I grinned at him. "When you do that, you will be writing. You will be putting words on paper. You will be producing. You will have begun the actual story-writing process."

A tiny light seemed to click on inside his brain. His mouth opened as he contemplated telling himself what his story was going to be and how it was going to unfold.

I went on, "Begin by writing something, let's say, about a man who finds the girl of his dreams and knows he will marry her. The problem is, she is engaged to the town's richest guy and really likes her situation. The hero can't understand why he can't get her away from this person and begins a campaign to win her to himself." My young friend's face was coming alive, "Then, spell out the entire plot so that you understand what your concept is and how it will unfold in the telling." I could see his eyes take on a faraway look and he was off in the world of fiction. I rehashed the idea of using a synopsis and outline and let him go. "As soon as you finish with any part of this piece, bring it by and let me see it."

About two weeks later the same young man stopped me again. This time he had several sheets of white paper with words typed on one side. The lines were double-spaced and the format looked good. He had the concept, a synopsis and a complete outline of his novel. "Now what do I do?" he asked. His grin was triumphant. He had overcome the first hurdle in his race to finish an entire story.

I advised him to begin his first draft.

"How?"

The first draft always begins with a scene which orients the reader with *time* and *place* and an *introduction of the lead character* as soon as possible. So, this young man's story may begin like this (fictitious byline):

A Struggle for Love

By Jay Scott

The silence of the evening placed a blanket of peace over the town of Mesa, Arizona. A slight breeze stirred a twist of dust around a slender young man as he stepped up onto the curb. He flipped a cigarette into the gutter near the corner and ambled along. His mouth felt as though a truck had run through it and he wished he hadn't even put the filter to his lips. The smoke had merely served to distract him from the dreaded confrontation with Dr. McClain. He really didn't smoke regularly anyway and he grimaced at the thought of the childish way he always handled things he didn't want to face. *Here I am, twenty-two and supposedly a mature male, and I'm acting like a teenager*, he thought. He grinned. *Well, this is the age of the eighties and if the women can do their thing, then so can men.* The idea made him chuckle aloud.

The lengthening shadows of the grey stone buildings cast a dark coolness across the sidewalk as he passed an open door. His deep concentration pulled a furrow into his brow. He didn't notice Lisa Kelly staring at him from her parked Ferrari. She called. "Jim." He didn't respond. "Oh, Mr. Wilsonnn," she cooed.

Jim jerked from his concentration, his eyes momentarily unfocused. Finally he caught sight of the red sports car. Lisa's long blonde hair and full red lips were accentuated by her white, puff-sleeved blouse. She was trouble and Jim knew it. He merely waved at her and smiled. When she saw he wasn't going to stop and talk with her, she started the engine of the small car and drove slowly along next to the curb. "You wanna ride?" she asked. Her voice was sultry and she tilted her head seductively as he glanced at her. He sighed a little and she laughed at the effect she had on him. "Come on," she urged. "Forget Pamela Parks and come with me. We'll have some grass and head for the open road."

Jim stopped. He looked down at her as she pulled the Ferrari to the curb. Its paint glistened in the waning daylight. He saw his own reflection in the polished fender. The girl leaned across the seat and opened the door on his side. Her low-cut blouse hung slightly open and she lingered for a moment. Her lips parted, and she wet them with her tongue. Jim's mouth opened and his breathing became labored. Lisa smiled, then sat up and patted the seat next to her. "Come on, Jimbo. The grass is waiting."

"I've got to go to the science lab and see Doc McClain about my finals," he said. "If I don't I won't get my degree."

Lisa cocked her head and laughed. "So, you'll have to do a little summer school." She patted the seat once more. "I'm going to be here all summer. We can start a strong relationship right now."

AN ANALOGY

Notice how the title of the above piece integrates with its opening to make a single statement of understanding. With this short opening, the time and place are easily understood and the major characters are introduced. Two of these characters are seen and the other one is mentioned. There are even some clues to the struggles this young man is having with his life. Let's take a look at the following breakdown and see what we've found out in this less than 400-word opening.

1. Time: Early evening in modern history. (The 1980s.)
2. Place: Mesa, Arizona, on a street in town.
3. Lead Character: Jim Wilson is a tall, slender college senior who is twenty-two years old.

4. Other Lead Characters: Lisa Kelly is a pretty blonde girl who has a seductive manner. She smokes grass and appears to be of loose moral character. The other girl mentioned is Pamela Parks. By the way she is introduced (by the other girl) the reader can assume she is Jim Wilson's girlfriend.

With brevity, the author has given the reader a full understanding of the time, place, protagonist, sub-protagonist and antagonist, along with a story line trend. Not bad. How did it all happen? It came about by the telling of a story.

The first thing a writer must do to begin telling the story is *begin telling the story*. That may seem like an oversimplification, but I assure you it isn't. There are too many writers who are like professional students: they will do everything there is to do to prepare for writing, but never actually begin the process. Professional students go to school to prepare for an actual job in the work force, but they never do get into the flow of employment. They just keep going to school to prepare some more. There is definitely a correlation between these two types of human beings. Both have the desire to *have been* whatever it is he or she admires. The professional student desires to *have been* a scientist, or a botanist, or a chemical engineer, but never becomes one because he can't quit going to school long enough to join the team on some project with an established company.

The novice author desires to *have been* published. He doesn't ever get around to preparation of the manuscript, research, outline, character sketches and studying the craft of writing. He talks about writing quite a bit though. In fact, his conversation is always centered around the book, article or short story he is supposedly writing. That conversation goes on for many years. I've met some writers (that's what they call themselves) who have been working on the same book for more than twenty years.

So, back to *square one*: Begin by beginning.

REVISION

After the first draft of the story has been completed, a reading is necessary. I suggest the writer read his manuscript aloud. It is always best if someone else is present during the reading. There is something about reading the work to someone else that brings out its flaws. It makes the dross rise to the top, where it's much easier to scrape it away. The idea of tossing away hundreds of words is heartrending to some authors, but judicious editing is a must. The words must be clear and concise. The sentences need to flow smoothly through each succeeding thought. Each paragraph must have smooth transitions. Each scene must paint a vivid word picture in order to transfer the mental image from the writer to the reader with high fidelity. Editing accomplishes these goals when it is done without considering the feelings of the writer, but the feelings of the reader only.

If the writer considers his own desires, he will leave in words which mean something to him, yet fail to transfer a concise mental image. He will not dig out those redundant phrases or cut away the words which fail to effectively join one scene or element in the story to another.

Editing hurts. One must bleed internally in order to cut his work and make it the best it can be.

REWRITING

Once your scalpel has carved out everything that isn't your best writing, your rewriting must follow the same pattern. Keep trimming away the fatty tissue clinging to the sides of your paragraphs. As the rewriting takes place, *better* words, phrases and sentences should be sought. Some authors can't bear to see those edited words fall away. They reestablish everything they have torn down, and all is lost.

CHAPTER FIVE

The "No!"-It-Alls

Authors have a distorted view of editors, probably because what view they do have is from the other side of a gigantic communication gap. The author doesn't understand the editor's job and considers him an ogre who simply stamps "No!" on everything that comes across his desk. The editor then promptly stuffs the author's manuscript into the return envelope with a form rejection slip and zips it back out of his office and into a waiting room. There it sits and grows mold while the author is at home wondering what has happened to it. That waiting room is the editor's way of making the author think he has taken the time and effort to read the submitted work.

Of course, this view is far from the truth. Let's take an unbiased look at the editor and see if we can understand him better.

The editor is not an ogre. He is a person with a job to do (usually he has dozens of jobs to do) and little time in which to perform his work to the best of his ability. He is adept at reading a manuscript quickly and can usually tell right away whether it has potential for his publishing house or should be returned. Both the author and the editor are needed to make the publishing world function. Each needs the other to survive.

In this chapter, we'll take a look at the author's side of his relationship with the editor. Later, we'll discover what the editor sees and how he views what comes across his desk.

THE LIBRARY

Since we've already been to the research desk at the library, gotten into the bound editions of the magazines and found the magazine section up front, let's take a different tack and move around the shelves and down the aisles.

Why go to the library when you want to get to know various editors? First, the magazines have the current editorial people listed on the masthead page and give the proper address of the editorial offices. Also, as an author, you'll have the opportunity to get to know the editor's personality by what he prints.

In the bookshelves, *Writer's Market* and *The Writer's Handbook* sit waiting to be used by the author who is diligent enough to search their pages and discover the wealth of information on book and magazine publishers (even the obscure ones are listed).

Then there's the card catalog with all its information about publishers and their books. The use of the card catalog is overlooked by too many authors. The research librarian will help you learn how to use the card system and thereby add to the usable tools of the writer.

Since storage and cost hinder the average person from owning several different sets of encyclopedias, the library is invaluable as a resource for anything you want to know.

BOOKSTORES

Many large chain bookstores have begun to carry books for the fringe customer. Books on writing are not best-sellers, but bookstores are carrying more books on the subject. These will help the new author in many areas, but certainly one of the major areas is that of understanding the relationship between the editor and the author.

When entering a bookstore, especially one of the large chain stores, note that there are usually "dumps" (cardboard display units) with full-color posters up front or near the cashier's counter. These well-advertised books are the "hot items" of the week or month. Some carry on for several months. At the time of this writing, *Jane Fonda's Workout Book* has been on the best-seller list for well over a year. So, the author who is aware of what is going on will stop and search these dumps and see what the trend is that fills these "hot spots" in the bookstores.

Many times a writer will have friends who watch for

books, magazines or news items for him and help him keep abreast of what is going on in the world of books. From these items and trends, the author can become instinctive about coming trends. Everything runs in a pattern, which follows with another pattern, and so on.

TO WHOM IT MAY CONCERN

After the author has decided to settle on a certain publishing house and has researched the editor's like and dislikes (by reading what the editor has published) and seems to have a "feel" for the entire concept, he can blow the whole thing by writing an amateurish query. *Always remember: that first letter is the editor's introduction to you, the writer.* That first letter to the editor can create a very strong relationship, or it can blow the whole thing. Too many authors fail to get the editor's name and title, and then fail to direct their letter to that person by name and title.

Just to give you an example: I recently received a letter addressed, *"To Whom It May Concern."* When I sent my rejection letter back to the individual, I began it with, *"To Whom It May Concern:* Your manuscript found no one who was concerned, so I'm returning it herewith."

I suppose one of the most important things to remember about dealing with people is that they are *people.* Even if one sits in a plush executive chair atop a big-city skyscraper and smokes two-dollar cigars, that individual is still a person with feelings. Each of us has similar hurts, similar problems, similar likes and dislikes. We are all basically alike. We are all "turned on" by similar things and "turned off" by similar negatives. If someone yells, "Hey, you!" you're turned-off. That's just the way it is. A letter from an author which begins with anything other than the editor's name and title has a very poor beginning.

So, *point one* in writing the query is: *Discover and use the editor's name and title.* (Spell it correctly.)

CATCHING FISH

Generally, writing is like catching fish. If there is no hook at the end of the line, there will be no fish in the boat.

For a writer, the query is like what my father called "chumming" the water. That is, tossing some sort of bait into the water to attract the fish so that they're ready to bite on what you throw in next.

In fishing there is no hook in the chum, but in writing, a hook is always present in exceptional writing — even in the query.

Let's take a look at a query. First we'll look at some opening lines. Here is how it should look (single-spaced).

Proper Date Here

Dear Mr. Noton:

I've discovered the beginnings of a new trend that your subscribers will want to know about. Since your magazine keeps a finger on the pulse of modern America, and you haven't covered this subject yet, I'd like to write it for you. The subject is . . .

Here are two opening lines which hook the editor's attention. Why? Because they are in tune with the magazine's slant and promise something for its subscribers. They generate enthusiasm and knowledge of the magazine. Since the author wants to please the editor's audience, the editor likes him and has a positive attitude as he reads the rest of the query. The author was careful to let the editor know he had kept abreast of his magazine and has studied several issues. That is important information and adds credibility to the author's professional status. The editor is pleased with anyone who exudes enthusiasm for his periodical. It appears the author reads the magazine regularly and found that the magazine was slanted toward his own inspired, new and fantastic idea. The editor wants it to be good so he can feel a part of the entire process. He will subconsciously think, *If the idea is good and it is well-written, I'm responsible.* So, he wants the author to succeed.

BREVITY

Now that the author has the attention of the editor, he can't drop the ball, or miss the idea behind the query. It is a *short introduction to the concept*.

Notice the two words, *short* and *introduction*. Short (in writing queries) means it should be a single page, single-spaced type with plenty of margins on all sides. At most, a query should not go beyond a page and a half, and that would be stretching it.

Within the query, the author's qualifications for writing the particular article, short story or book should be given. Going on about credits which do not actually enhance your qualifications for that single proposal will cause the editor to feel you can't quiet talking about yourself.

Now about the word *introduction*: That's all a query is. It does not have to go on and on about the concept, only introduce it. The following is one of the finest examples I could find of an actual query from one of the subscribers to our magazine. It was obvious she had studied our periodical before querying me.

Date

Thomas A. Noton
Editor
P.O. Box 5650
Lakeland, FL 33803

Dear Mr. Noton:

I broke into writing through the how-to article. I believe your readers would find help and insight into getting into print through my article: "How To Break Into Print The How-To Way."

I spent two years crying over rejection slips until it occurred to me that I might use my familiarity with crochet to some advantage. (Write about what you know best.) I had sold one design, so I composed and mailed an article on "How To Design Your Own Patterns." It sold immediately, along with another design. My first sale! I was delighted. To date I have sold five such articles and have two columns on designing patterns in national magazines. I also do a book review column for a crochet magazine twice a year (on assignment).

Breaking into print through a hobby could be the encouragement a beginning writer needs. I remember I was so frustrated that I thought a writer had to know someone to get into this business. My budding crochet career gave me the experience and encouragement to persevere toward my chosen field, fiction. Now my first novel has been accepted. It all began because I wrote a how-to. I believe my article will help others to do the same.

Sincerely,

Aggie Villanueva

Notice the points of Mrs. Villanueva's query:
1. Used and spelled the editor's name and title correctly.
2. Hooked the editor's attention with the first two sentences.
3. Kept it short (about 200 words) and clear.
4. Gave her qualifications within the context of the concept.
5. Stopped when she had stated her objective.

Since I am the editor/publisher of a magazine which is designed to teach writing, Aggie grabbed my attention by telling me how she got into writing. She added the fact that she was willing to share it with my readers. Hey, these readers are my "children" in spirit. If someone wants to help them and has what it takes, she's won my approval. So, after she said she wanted to help my readers, she gives me the details of what brought her to the conclusion that she had something to give them. She did so by telling me she understands one of the first principles of writing: *Write about what you know best.* She added the idea that this first sale wasn't a fluke — it happened five times, and she has written for national magazines.

When she added the fact that she receives assignments from these publications, that really iced the cake. When she said, " . . . could be the encouragement a beginning writer needs. I remember I was so frustrated that . . ." she told me she really has a heart to help others overcome the frustrations of rejection. Finishing with a success story is top-notch query writing. "Now my first novel has been accepted. It all began because I wrote a how-to. I believe my article will help others to do the same." The last three sentences caused me to stop everything and write a short note to this lady and tell her to get on the stick and get that article to me right away. (It was published in our November '82 issue.)

PART TWO
THE
EDITOR

That person (or persons) receiving the author's manuscript for evaluation, acceptance or rejection, and editing.

CHAPTER SIX

A New Day

From an author's perspective, the editorial office is one of the most misunderstood places. In the author's vivid imagination, the picture reflects a den of iniquity, a place where lions roam free to chew up manuscripts, or possibly a dungeon complete with rack for torturing the writers until they work without payment.

In order to dispel the misconceptions about editors and their offices, we'll take a guided tour through a typical magazine publisher's office. On our way, we'll stop and look over the shoulder of each staff member.

Before we do that, let's take one last look at the

imaginary editor's office and the man behind the desk. His office door is made of dark wood with a frosted glass window. The name of the publishing firm is painted in fancy gold letters across the glass. As we enter the office, we spot a slight, elderly man with thin wisps of grey hair protruding from under his perspiration-stained visor. He is sitting in an old chair examining one of the many scrubby manuscripts piled on one edge of his desk. An oil lamp affords the only light in the room. The stench of cigar smoke comes from the soggy stub stuck in the side of his mouth. A dirty coffee cup half filled with cold coffee sits at his elbow, and his wire-rimmed glasses have slipped down on his nose. The lamp on his desk flickers, casting eerie shadows on the wall. An old black typewriter sits on a dark metal stand at his right, and a broken-spined dictionary is lying next to it. For heat in the colder months, an iron radiator clanks itself into some semblance of life. The summer brings stifling heat. A single open window serves as relief. With the editor working under conditions like this, it's no wonder he uses a large rubber rejection stamp with a thick, red ink pad.

Since the editor and his office in the foregoing scene is simply a figment of some authors' imaginations, we'll now take a look at the real thing.

IT'S THE REAL WORLD

The typical work days begins at nine in the morning. Several things happen at once. There is a receptionist who may serve as a secretary and mail opener. She actually receives the mail and zips it open, piling each piece according to its destination: queries and manuscripts to editorial, subscriptions to that department, advertising to the ad office, etc.

While the mail is being opened, the senior editor may be having a meeting with the entire staff. He (or she) may get each of the department heads together in the morning for a session on planning the day, talking about a future issue, or working out yesterday's problems.

Once all the mail is opened and distributed to the proper departments and the editors' meeting has been adjourned, the work begins.

MANUSCRIPT DESTINATIONS

We'll follow the editorial mail. The pile of manuscripts (for larger publishers, that may mean bags of mail) come to the editorial office by various means and in myriad shapes and sizes. The editor prefers that manuscripts be sent flat when there are more than a few pages. The author places the manuscript in a large envelope (9" by 12") with another envelope (self-addressed and stamped with proper postage) folded and tucked inside with an 8½" by 11" piece of cardboard to keep the package flat and neat in mailing. Whether the author sends the manuscript first class, third class or even special fourth class is of no concern to the editor. It is a matter of economics for the author. Registered or certified mail will not endear the author to the editor, and since the author is merely sending a photocopied manuscript, insured mail isn't necessary.

The receptionist carries the stack of mail to the first desk in the editorial office. That office is well lighted, and the person behind the desk may be a college student who is majoring in English or journalism and is doing some graduate work. Her job is to sort the mail. She spends the morning putting the manuscripts into stacks according to several criteria. If the material is obviously not for that publisher, it goes into the rejection basket and is returned forthwith.

This *junior editor* or *assistant editor* is responsible to see that the material requested by the editor gets to his desk. That is material which has been assigned by him. The junior editor also determines which queries are to go on to another editorial person with more authority and which are to be given a form rejection. This young person is gaining valuable experience by dealing with the material that comes through the door (formerly "over the transom") of the editorial office.

MOVING DOWN THE LINE

Beyond the first desk is another desk. It may be a bit larger and even have a copy machine nearby. The person behind that desk may be called the *associate editor* or *managing editor*. His job entails, in part, looking at and deciding what to do with the mail the junior editor passes on to him. The stack of mail consists of queries, full manuscripts or partial manuscripts. His job is to sort out what may be useful for a current issue or may have the potential to meet some future need. He divides the stack into piles according to what each pile represents and delivers those which he sees as valuable to another editorial member, usually "the" editor.

THE STACK STOPS HERE

Since there are few manuscripts left in the pile, the editor doesn't have to be concerned with whether the material is relevant for his magazine or not. That has already been determined by a competent staff member. The editor's job is to determine (by very subjective means) whether he likes each manuscript or query. What he has in his hands are only *potential* acceptances. After scanning each submission, the editor usually determines (by that scanning) whether or not he wants to take a more thorough look at the piece. If he decides he's seen enough, he may simply attach a form rejection to it. He may even scratch a note to the author, giving personal instructions or encouragement. He may *feel* like doing that many times, but time usually disallows it.

To those articles or stories he deems usable, he attaches a slip instructing his secretary to make copies of each for the editorial committee meeting.

THE FINAL TEST

Everyone on the editorial staff receives a copy of the day's catch, and is asked to read as much of the material as time allows. An editorial meeting is set up to discuss the manuscripts' merits and liabilities. Each manuscript is carefully "talked out" and a determination is made at that time. For those manuscripts or queries that get to the committee and are rejected, there is usually a nice letter which accompanies the rejected piece. It may begin with, "I really like this piece, but . . ." The encouragement or criticism given by an editor can affect career decisions for many new authors.

Manuscripts accepted for the current issue are edited. The *current* issue is the one being worked on at the time, but it may not appear on the newsstands for several months. Editors work well in advance.

The editor may do some of the actual editing, but

much of it is often done by an associate editor or assistant editor. Most senior editors like to take a final look to be certain the editing is done according to the publisher's policies.

Once the editing is complete, a retyping may be necessary. If it is, a secretary performs that function. Many manuscripts go directly to the typesetter with the editorial corrections on them. After the manuscript has been typeset, the editor or one of his staff proofreads the material to see that it is absolutely correct.

In the meantime, if the publication *pays on acceptance*, the editor has issued a voucher to the business office and a check is readied for his signature or that of the publisher. Payment on acceptance is a common practice with top magazines, though many smaller magazines pay only after actual publication. The pay may be a flat fee for the article or a certain amount per printed word. Either way, the author is happy and the magazine is happy. Both are able to exist a while longer.

78- THE EDITORIAL DOOR

CHAPTER SEVEN

Stretching the Day

When the editor arrives at the office each morning, he must outline the day's activities. Since he is almost always understaffed and faced with a mountainous workload, he must stretch his hours to their limits. He must keep in mind the current needs of his publishing house and at the same time look to future needs.

Let's take an example of a female editor running a moderately successful women's magazine designed to meet the needs of career women between the ages of twenty-five and thirty-six who have had at least two years of college. They are generally self-supported, or could be if they so chose. The subscribers to this magazine are style conscious, with a high standard of living.

The editor must understand what affects the thinking and emotions of women with these characteristics. So, keeping abreast of current trends and styles is part of this editor's job. She must read the publications of her contemporaries and stay in touch with the fashion section of the larger newspapers. The editor who fails to read, watch, and discover what is going on in the world around her will soon be unemployed.

After planning her day, the editor may begin with a time of reading (scanning) the larger newspapers and other women's magazines. She may place the editorial meeting in second priority, jotting down the discoveries she's made in the mornings's perusal for discussion. At the editorial meeting, she may compile current projects which meet the future needs of her readers and fit the ever-changing format of her magazine. (Everything concerning women is changing rapidly, so an editor must be alert to those changes and move with them.)

After the editorial meeting, she may schedule time to respond to the many queries and manuscripts which have filtered down to her desk. Those she has a definite penchant for she sets aside for a more extensive reading and possible acceptance. Acceptance entails the securing of rights, sending a memo to the accounting office and making copies to distribute to the editorial staff for copy editing.

The editor is responsible to oversee the entire editorial staff. She must make decisions quickly and accurately. That same person must be diplomatic in responding to the advertising manager who has just sold a four-page spread for which no room is available, but wants to "bump" (delete) a feature article so his ad can fit into the coming issue.

For all she is worth, the editor tries yet seldom succeeds in finishing work far in advance of a deadline.

With a workload as heavy as this, it's easy to see why many queries and manuscripts are not recognized with a letter directly from the editor. Instead, the author receives a slip of paper with a mass-printed message and a rubberstamp signature. The editorial staff is so busy putting the accepted material together, editing it and setting up the "dummy" magazine, then stripping in fillers, advertising space and regular columns that they don't have time to write extensive rejection slips or fancy acceptance letters.

So, the author who understands what is going on at the editorial level has patience. In order to cope with the extended delay of his submitted article or story, the diligent writer begins a new project — forgetting the one in the mail. That allows the editor the time necessary to do the job for which she was hired.

84- THE EDITORIAL DOOR

SHOVING A FOOT IN THE DOOR -85

CHAPTER EIGHT

Shoving a Foot in the Door

Since queries are so important to getting your foot in the editorial door, this chapter is dedicated to the query as the editor sees it. Since he's the one we are trying to impress with our queries, it would be good to see what he thinks about them.

I received a query recently that prompted me to respond with the following letter. As an editor I receive a pile of letters to which I respond candidly about the author's ability to get my attention and obtain a positive response. This letter, however, was a flagrant violation of all that is sensible when writing to an editor. My response gives enough understanding of its content to warrant my not publishing the letter itself.

> Dear (author's name):
> I once asked a girl to the prom and was rejected. The girl in question was very upset at the way I had posed my request. I simply stated, "I've asked nearly every other girl in school to go to the prom with me, but they've all said 'no,' so I thought I'd ask you."
> Is there any doubt as to the reason she turned me down? Well, it's the same with this request you've sent. You state, "I've tried different magazines without success ... (so I thought I'd) send this to you ..."
> I'll have to say, you need help in the basics of getting an editor's favorable response. I suggest you subscribe to our magazine if you ever want to be published. You'll learn the basics and then some. I don't guarantee you'll be published after you begin receiving our magazine, but, if you take to heart what our editorial staff is saying, you'll be a whole lot closer.
> Sincerely,
>
> Thomas A. Noton
> Editor/Publisher

The letter this author had sent me would insult any editor, even as I had insulted the girl I'd asked to the prom. What *I* saw in what the author wrote and what *she* saw in what she wrote were two different things. Whenever you write to an editor, put yourself in his place as you reread what you've written. If there are any sentences which may give the wrong impression, delete them or at least rewrite them.

As an editor, I've seen far too many queries and cover letters which leave me feeling useless. I wonder how the person could develop such assumptions about writing. Then I think back. I too was ignorant of the craft. I too thought that a writer was someone who sat down at a typewriter and pounded out anything that came to him and sent it off to the first editor who came in mind. I too assumed that I needed no formal training, no format or procedure. *Hey,* I thought, *I can construct sentences. I can spell fairly well. I know a noun from a verb. I've certainly read stuff I know I could write as well or better.*

So, this chapter is dedicated to showing you what *not* to do when writing to an editor. Whether you are sending a query or a cover letter with your manuscript, be careful not to fall into these areas of failure.

LETTERS I'VE CRIED OVER

This first one was typed (that's the only thing it had going for it) on flimsy white paper. Other than that, it was — well, read it for yourself.

Dear Ma'am, or Sir,
I'm sending you a copy of one of my stories and I want to know if it is good or not because I have had this dream of becoming a writer for along time but I never did any thing about it before until some of my dear friends told me that I should do something about my stories because they were to good to keep to myself so I would like to know if my one story is any good or not it really

won't hurt my feelings none if yous tell me that my stories aren't any good because most of my family tell me I'm only living on a pipe dream but this is my only chance to see if I'm any good as a writer or not if not I'll stop writing because I don't like to waste time and the money buying paper.
Yours Very Truly,

There are so many errors in this letter that it would take too much space to point out all of them. First, the editor's name and title must be used. Proper punctuation is a must. This 148-word sentence had no punctuation and contained many misspelled words and grammatical errors. It nearly made me weep.

It is not difficult to see that this person needs to learn the *basic* basics before she attempts to write another word. How does an editor respond to someone like this? It's a tough job.

From time to time I receive letters from people who know they've got just what every editor wants:

To Whom It May Concern:
My autobiography is up for sale.
At this time, you have the opportunity to become the publisher of my book. If you're willing to read it thoroughly, then you may contact me. Because of the contents of my book, only those truly sincere in publishing it will have the opportunity to have a copy of the manuscript.
I'll expect your answer immediately.
Sincerely,

First, autobiographies from unknowns are usually

boring. Who are they that anyone would be interested in their lives? Sure, they've had troubles, tragedies, problems and even catastrophes, but their lives aren't much different from that of the guy next door. So, an autobiography from an unknown author receives very little attention and generates no excitement.

Look at the nerve of the above author. He comes across as though the entire publishing industry should scream, "Stop the presses! We have an opportunity to look at *the book of the century!*" That just isn't going to happen.

The dictator-style query is doomed from its opening line. Surely an author can get an editor's attention with a professional presentation and a good reader hook faster than he can by gestapo-style intimidation.

The next letter was handwritten and went like this:

To Whom It May Concern:
I can't remember how I got your address. I think I got it last year, I'm not sure. Anyway, the reason I got it was to send it on to my cousin in Nebraska who wants to be a writer in the worst way. I was going to send it to her but I never did. She gave up the idea anyway.

Since then, I had a baby girl. She was 7 pounds and 3 ounces. Real cute and loveable too. It was my first child and it was a real neat experience. I was so excited about it that my husband said I should write about it. Well, I thought about it and decided it would be a good thing to do. I could tell other women what a neat experience it is to have a baby. I think I'll make it into a book with pictures of her and me and Fred (that's my husband) and it will be a thrill for everyone who reads it. They can look at the cute pictures too. It will sell real well.

How do I go about doing it? Will you send me a letter and tell me what to do and how to go about doing this?

Thanks,

Here is a lady who presumes that a book about her experience of having a baby will be so unique that it will "thrill" the readers. She also presumes this task is so simple that an editor could explain the process to her in a letter.

SENDING THE CARE PACKAGE

Never send self-published work with your query. Unless requested, don't send examples of your previously published work with your query. Simply state your accomplishments within the body of the letter. Don't do what this person did.

Dear Sir:

I wasn't sure you published poetry or not, but I thought I'd send my book of poetry to you so you could see the kind of stuff I write and publish myself. I'll let you use any of it you want to. You can send a check to me at the address on the back of the book. If you don't publish poetry, then I missed it with this shot-in-the-dark didn't I? Well, anyway, I tried.

Sincerely,

Whew! When I read letters like that and receive the accompanying self-published books, I wonder what kind of person has such funds available that he or she can afford to squander money on self-publishing, then send out copies as shots-in-the-dark. More than that, I wonder what sort of writer would expect results from such methods.

This next letter is typical of many potential writers. Note the dirty keys.

> Dear Mr. Noton:
> We have a club of women who meet a few times a month to talk about writing and read about it. None of us have actually come down to really writing anything of value as yet, because we all admit we can't sit down at work at it.
> Well, I finally wrote this short piece. If you publish it I'll be happy. I'll be the only one in our group with an actual published article. Won't you make me happy?
> Sincerely,

Can you believe this lady actually admits she (and her friends) won't work at her craft, then turns around and pleads for an editorial handout? She wants to be able to show off to the others in her group. I can assure her that she'll never get published through childish pleading. Along with the content of such a letter, the dirty keys only further guarantee the failure of a non-author who will remain a non-author unless she begins to seriously study and work at her craft.

Here's another one for the books. (That's just a

figure of speech. This person won't be getting published any time soon.)

Dear Friends,

I received your address to your magazine or publishing company (I'm not certain what you actually do) through another person. That person said you would probably be interested in my type of work. I'm unclear as to what type of work you wish to see, but he said you publish my style stuff. It would be good for both of us if we could get together. I know you would benefit from my writings. Everything I write is real good so you should be pleased with it.

What do you think?

Yours Truly,

This letter produced one question for me: *What do I think about what?*

The following letter looked as though it had been typeset and printed at a local quick-print shop.

ATTENTION PUBLISHER:

I have written this great little short dramatic love story and find myself looking for a publisher for it. Hey, it's real good and I'm proud of it. But, after sending it to several publishers, your name was given to me as a possible source for this new and fascinating material.

I've enclosed a postcard for your favorable reply.

Thanks,

The postcard:

```
_____YES!  Rush  your  exciting
story to us at once!
Signed:    _____
Editor: _____
Comments:
```

Such requests are unprofessional. The editor has too many demands on his life as it is. He certainly won't take kindly to more pressure being applied by an unskilled author.

The following is my reply to a cover letter and manuscript I received recently.

Dear (author's name):
   Please forgive me for making the judgment I'm about to make, but I must look at material sent to us and judge the writer's ability by it. Your work lacks professional appearance. Your manuscript is on onionskin paper, folded beyond recognition, typed over in spots and has whiteout and a staple in it. It fails to have any semblance of professional format. There is no title to the work and no byline.
   I'm sorry, but we don't look twice at a submission like this. Please take this admonition in the true spirit of concern for your writing abilities.
   Since no editor would take a second look at this

type of submission, why not create professional-looking work, indicative of a professional writer?
Sincerely,

Thomas A. Noton
Editor/Publisher

Finally, I received this letter.

Dear Mr. Noton:
Before you reject this manuscript, give me a second, please? You rejected my last effort with a tough letter. You said I would be upset about it and I was. I also laughed.

I hate to admit it, but you were right on every count. I had missed the mark completely. Now, if you'll take a few minutes and read this article, you'll see how well I've learned from you. If I still need your rebuke, send it on, but if you think (as I do) it's a publishable piece, then I hope you'll accept it.
Sincerely,
(This writer has learned by taking criticism wisely.)

Generally, I find editors to be people who wish they had the time to tell writers what really counts with them. When an editor has taken his precious time to comment on an author's work, then receives a letter back saying how much the author learned, the editor's day is made. That's especially true if the author proves how much has been gained by submitting a catchy cover letter like the last one. Certainly, that author had my attention. That's what cover letters and queries are supposed to do. So top-notch writers must make their queries hook the editor's attention with strong, relevant statements. Give the editor your most professional work. Use his or her name and title. Study the publishing houses. Look for their style and slant before you submit a query. Get sample copies and writer's guidelines from monthly publications. Send for guidelines from book publishers. Buy a copy of *Writer's Market*.

POTPOURRI

1. Never address your letter to a non-person by using: *To Whom It May Concern, Dear Sir or Madam, Dear Editor,* or *Publishers.*

2. Never send in anything that is handwritten. Queries should be single-spaced, typewritten on 16- or 20-pound bond paper. *Don't use onion skin, thin paper or erasable bond.*

3. Never use pastels or fancy papers. Plain white is the only acceptable paper used by professionals.

4. Never type on the back of the page. Queries should be typed on one side of one page.

5. Never send a query without enclosing an SASE.

6. Never submit a query without a succinct list of your qualifications.

7. Never ask general questions, like: "What do you need for your publishing house?" Those questions prove you're not a professional.

8. Never tell the editor how your family and friends feel about your writing. Their recommendation means nothing.

9. Never send the editor a separate biographical sheet with a query. The bio sheet comes later.

10. Never begin your query with anything that will give the editor the feeling you haven't seen his latest publication. Don't begin with, "Last year I heard that..."

11. Never submit anything with smudges from dirty keys, coffee cups or jelly sandwiches.

12. Never indicate that the submission you propose is your first attempt at writing, or that you've attempted many times but haven't yet been accepted for publication. Allow your query and your manuscript to stand (or fall) on its own merit.

13. Never write long sentences. Keep them short and to the point.

14. Never send the material before you receive a response from your query.

PART THREE
THREE
THE PUBLISHER

That person (or persons) actually underwriting the publishing process to take the manuscript to its intended audience.

CHAPTER NINE

The Publishing House

When the average person thinks of a publishing house, he envisions a ritzy New York firm with a suite of offices atop a huge workroom filled with printing presses. That is not reality.

Few publishing houses actually print their own material, since it's much less expensive to have a commercial printer do it. In fact, all of the typesetting, layout and design, printing and binding are usually done by "jobbers" — businesses specializing in those fields, and who have been contracted by the publisher.

Let's take a look at what happens to your manuscript after it has been read and edited by an editor in a publishing house.

Copies of the manuscript are made for the various contractors. One copy will go to the typesetter, where it is set in the type size and style determined in a meeting of the editor and the layout and design people. The typesetter works with a computerized machine which types, spaces, adjusts and generally sets the type in the manner prescribed by the staff of the publishing house.

In the smaller operations, the editor or his assistant may actually put the edited material in his car and take it to the typesetter a few miles away. There, they work together getting the edited material on sheets of heavy card stock, called "boards." The boards are then photographed with a special camera, and the negatives are used to create positive metal plates. The plates are used to actually lift the ink from rollers on the printing press and print it on sheets of paper, which will be bound together to make a magazine or book.

While the typesetting is going on, the layout and design department does the artwork to be used with the "copy" to be printed. For a book, this entails jacket design, art (if any) to be used at the beginning of each chapter, photographs for the author's biographical blurb, posters, advertising material and many other details.

A copy of the manuscript will also go to the advertising copy writing department. This department must work closely with the layout and design people. The advertising copy and artwork must enhance each other and cause the reader to buy the product.

With the larger publishing house, the wheels move much more slowly. There is always extra paperwork to be done before the book can be sent on to another department for further work.

The one-man office is quite different. One major publishing house that I know of began operation in the back bedroom of the publisher's home. When the publisher is the editor, the copyboy and the janitor, he spends sixteen to eighteen hours a day at work and gets a lot done. By the time his publishing venture has blossomed to a place where he can move to an office and hire someone to edit, he knows more than he cares to about the business.

I got a smell of printer's ink in my nostrils when I was seventeen. I worked for a small printer-publisher in our little Florida town of Largo. At that time, Largo had a total population of about 3500. *The Largo Sentinel* was a weekly newspaper of about eight pages. The publisher was the editor, the staff writer (although he had others, too) and general overseer of the printing business. He saw to it that the stock room was supplied with paper and ink, and generally kept an eye on everything. He had a pressroom foreman, but he also had a large window in his office and a wide view of the press operation, including the typesetters and even the floor sweeper (me).

When news day arrived and the big press was cranked up to get the newspaper printed, all other work stopped. Everyone put down whatever he was doing and began to wrap papers for mailing. It was my job to get those bundles of papers down to the post office before it closed. Rolling, binding, labeling and stamping the weekly *Sentinel* was everyone's job. the boss saw to it that everyone pitched in and got it done.

As Largo has grown, the newspaper has grown with it. *The Largo Sentinel* now boasts 20,000 readership under the direction of a new owner. Although it is still a weekly, it has taken on a conservative political air and is used to sway thinking in the little West-Central Florida town.

So, we see that the publisher who cannot afford to have a fancy facility with plenty of office space and editorial help may find he has to hire a free-lance editor and contract out the printing, layout and design.

WHAT THEN IS A PUBLISHER?

The publisher is *one who makes public*. He or she is a person who believes in a cause, finances that cause and stands at the hub of the publishing wheel to see that each aspect is pulled together in proper order.

Let's develop a hypothetical situation. We'll say there's a man who decides that there aren't enough people around who understand how to use computers. That man meets others who agree with him. They form a limited partnership and put up $50,000 to finance a publishing venture. We'll also say that none of the partners knows anything about publishing except the man with the original idea. The others are just investors.

This one-man publishing house advertises in a big-city newspaper for people who can translate "computereze" into common language, and for a free-lance editor who can take the material and edit it into a readable book. After finding the right people, the work begins and the people are paid a fair wage for their efforts. The final manuscript is delivered to the publisher (the man with the original idea) and he contracts an artist with layout and design experience to do a jacket and a few pen and ink drawings to enhance the text. In the meantime, the publisher takes a copy of the edited work to a typesetter whom he will contract on a per-page rate. The type style and size is determined, and the manuscript is typeset accordingly.

The publisher then delivers the finished artwork for the jacket to a color separator who separates the colors on the artwork into red, yellow, blue and black. He has half-tones or line-shots (photo printing procedures) made of the pen and ink drawings and delivers the finished work to the camera room or a printer.

The camera and paste-up people shoot negatives,

make plates and "work up" the book for the pressroom.

Finally, through his contact with the printer, the publisher located a bindery to handle the book's binding. After the printing is complete, the bindery puts the color cover and the "guts" of the book together with heavy glue (for paperback) and trims the three sides for a final, finished look.

What has the publisher had to do with all this? He created the idea, and brought together all the elements to make a book a reality.

Now that the book is stacked in a warehouse, what can be done to get it out to the public? After all, the publisher had an idea that the general public needed a simple book about computers, so he must follow through and get the book out to the general public.

The publisher has to sell the idea of distributing the book to a national distributor. There are many distributors in the United States; some are good and some are not. The good ones distribute to a great many bookstores. When the top distributors take on a new book, they want to know what will happen to it. They don't want their books to collect dust in their customers' stores. They want titles that move. So, the publisher must assure the distributor that he has adequate advertising revenue to make the title move, or that the title is such a hot item that it will move if it is placed in "floor dumps" (cardboard display units) in the stores.

AND AFTER THAT?

If the publisher is successful with this first book, he will soon receive manuscripts from writers all over the world. Many will not interest him, but there will be a few which will spark his imagination and make him want to go all-out to publish them. When that happens, he has become a full-fledged publisher and must either buy the manuscript outright or contract with the author for payment on a royalty basis. Either way, the entire process begins all over again. Financing comes first, then the other processes will follow.

WOMEN IN PUBLISHING

There is no doubt that women have come into their own in many fields, and the publishing field has discovered its share of successful women. The list of female authors who have found success could make up a book in itself. Jane Fonda is an example. Women's magazines number their subscribers in the millions. *Ms.* is one of them.

Diet books, novels, recipe books, exercise books, textbooks and how-to books are just some of the areas of publishing open to women writers.

There is an endless list of editorial positions filled by competent women. If these positions didn't have such a high attrition rate, we might be able to list some of the women who have changed the world of publishing and editing. But changes in editorial positions are not limited to women in the field; men have an extremely high rate of editorial job-hopping.

FALLING INTO IT

I remember one story that has made the rounds of publishers' offices. It goes like this: It seems there was a young woman who thought she had discovered the secret of losing weight without mental or physical pain. She jotted down a synopsis of her proposed book and sent it to several major publishers. All of them turned her down with form rejection slips. She knew she had a diet book people everywhere would gobble up (so to speak), and for which they'd pay a high price. So she decided to publish the book herself. She went to a local printer and asked how much it would cost to get her book into print. The printer gave her several options. She decided to go first class and give it all she had. Since the book was being coauthored with a professional, the woman had to come up with thousands of dollars to pay the author, the printer, the typesetter, the artist, the color separator and the binder of the book.

Once she had 5,000 copies of the finished book, she had no room in her garage for her car. The difficult part had begun. Now she had to distribute these excellent books. She checked with a well-known distributor and found they wouldn't touch self-published material. In desperation, she contacted a state-circulated magazine and placed a small ad in its pages. The ad brought a modicum of results. She took the money she received and put it back into another (larger) ad. With the money she received from that second ad, she bought a small ad in a national magazine. That ad brought big results. She increased the size of her ad and a flood of mail (with checks enclosed) covered her dining table. Within a couple of months she had to go back to the printer for more books.

By the time she was fifty, that woman was running a publishing company worth "mega-bucks."

Although that doesn't happen often, it happens often enough to keep writers hoping.

VANITY PRESSES

Vanity presses are those printing companies (or publishers, as they call themselves) who prey on the conceit of the person who thinks he has something to tell the world. In far too many cases, the author pays outrageous prices to have his work printed and winds up with a roomful of books he can't get rid of no matter how hard he tries.

I was one of the authors at an autograph party not too many years ago. The other two authors were published by vanity presses. I overheard them talking. One lady said, "Who printed your book?" The other lady named the company. The first one responded with, "Oh, I didn't know they printed books. I had mine done by ..." and she named the company who printed her book with its pink cover. They both looked at me. "Who printed *your* book?" the first one asked.

I lowered my head, self-conscious. "I didn't have mine printed," I said. "My book was published by a publishing company in Nashville."

"What did you have to pay them?" she asked.

I smiled. "Ma'am, they paid me several thousand dollars for the right to publish my book. I didn't pay them. They paid me."

The two women stood there with their mouths open and stared at me. Finally, the second lady spoke. "You mean you didn't pay to have your book published?" She couldn't believe it.

I smiled and shook my head. "They flew my wife and me to their home office, put us up in a nice hotel, fed us sumptuously and contracted for my book." I couldn't resist adding more as I noted the look of envy on their faces. "I'm paid a royalty against the healthy advance."

The conversation suddenly excluded me. One lady turned to the other and said, "Well now, I do get a percentage of book sales." They turned away from me and sat down, talking to each other as though I didn't exist. I continued to eavesdrop. "I paid $3500 for 2500 copies."

The other one admitted that she had paid $4235 for

3500 copies of her book. The first lady clarified the price and structuring of her printing situation: "Well, I've only gotten 250 copies so far, but the other 2250 are being distributed overseas for me and I'll be paid a royalty on them."

I smirked and thought, *Fat chance.* How could that lady have any way of checking on the distribution of those fantasy copies? What may have happened is, the publisher took one look at the manuscript and figured this lady would be able to get rid of about 100 copies of the book, and he'd print 250 just to be sure. He then zapped her for $3500 and told her the rest would be distributed overseas. She'd get a royalty *if* they sold within a certain time (say one year). After that, the fine print in the contract could relieve the printer from any further obligation to the author and the printer has $3500 for a 250-copy printing.

As a famous king once said, "Vanity, vanity, all is vanity."

THE TYCOON CHAIRMAN OF THE BOARD

Since we've already stated that the average person envisions the publishing house as a suite of offices atop the actual printing facility, it is no wonder the average citizen sees the publisher as a cigar smoking, fat-jowled, mucketymuck who makes three or four hundred thousand dollars a year while hitting the ball off the first tee three times a week.

It's a very unusual publisher who has the time to pay much golf at all. Most publishers are men and women who chafe in frustration as they oversee the world of odds and ends that make up the full spectrum of the publishing game. They are people with their sleeves rolled up, who will sweep the floor when it's needed, take out the trash or lick stamps. They sweat out each deadline, put up with the high-strung editorial people and harden themselves against the outbursts of authors who feel they've gotten the short end of the editorial stick.

In short, publishers are the people who hold this business together and make it all work. Without the publisher, there would be no publishing business, no libraries, no bookstores, no greeting cards, no newspapers, no magazines, nothing to read at all.

THE ALL-IN-ONE COMPANY MAN

The publisher is the person who has every facet of the company in his hand. He pulls all the strings at the right time so that a smooth operation will bring together a fine product. (Well, that's the way it's *supposed* to go, anyway.)

He's the person who makes sure that there's someone to fetch the mail from the post office, open it and distribute it to the proper departments. He may not oversee that duty himself, but he has someone who does oversee it and gets back to him if it isn't running smoothly.

He hires a senior editor and gives that editor the right to interview underlings and (under supervision) hire a junior editor. In larger houses, there are senior editors, junior editors, managing editors, executive editors, associate editors and assistant editors. (And let's not forget the assistant to the assistant.) The jobs attached to each of these titles escape most of us. Each house has its own job description for the title.

The publisher oversees the editorial board meetings and gives input during these meetings to keep everyone's understanding of the other departments in perspective. Sometimes one department head begins to think the whole publishing mechanism hinges on his department.

The publisher directs his attention to the fact that it takes everyone working together to bring about the final product. He's upset when the final product is not perfect. He gets tight around the jaws when he reads a misspelled word, a typo or a grammatical error in one of his published pieces. He hires proofreaders to see to it that those errors don't make their way into his final products. When one of those errant portions is found by the publisher, the *faux pas* brings on screams that reverberate throughout the editorial office. The growls of the editor then echo in the proofreader's room, and everyone knows heads will roll.

ENHANCEMENT

The publisher hires the best he can afford in layout and design, artistic ability and photography. Finally, he contracts the finest color separators and printers in his price range. Even after all that, the product is never up to the perfection he desires, and he's upset.

He goes to the printer, who says the problem is with the color separator. He can't get the true color until the separator gives it to him. The separator says that the person to blame is the photographer. The photographer returns the blame to the printer.

What's a publisher to do?

He must coordinate all the elements in such a way that perfection (his definition of it) is reached. It is up to the publisher to hire the right people to do the job the way he envisions it.

Since the publisher hires everyone, including the editor, that editor is always looking for authors who can produce the type of material that will make his job more secure. Not that the publisher is standing over him with a double-bladed axe, but there is no doubt that the publisher and the editor want to keep the business in the black so they will keep themselves off of skid row.

The publisher has a simple job. First, he must take all the risk. Then, he merely comes up with the original financing, plans the production, hires the right editorial people, hires the advertising and promotions personnel, makes certain the layout and design people can give him the kind of artwork needed, sees that the copy is properly typeset and proofed, contracts the printers, contracts a subscription fulfillment service, contracts a distributor and does about fifty other jobs all within a given deadline.

PART
FOUR
THE AGENT

That person (or persons) filling the gap between the author and editor.

CHAPTER TEN

The Agent

Which is a tougher nut to crack, the editor or the agent? Both are really tough if they're worth their weight in twenty-pound bond. It's just as hard to get a good agent in your corner as it is to get an editor to give you a positive response.

I suppose the reason for this is that agents, like editors, are beseiged with sloppy, errant manuscipts from authors who believe they have birthed a wonder-child.

Just as most editors won't take a full manuscript without a query first, so the agent won't take on a new client without either a recommendation from one of his established clients or a reading fee paid to him by the author.

The largest literary agency in the world, Scott Meredith Literary Agency, Inc., of New York, charges hundreds of dollars to read large manuscripts from unpublished authors. (Many agencies follow that policy.) Reading fees are much less for shorter works. They'll waive the fees for authors who have been published a couple of times in major publications or have had a book published by a major publisher (usually within the past year). Scott Meredith's wording on that point in *Writer's Market* is a bit vague: "If a writer ... has begun to make major national magazine or TV sales with some regularity, we drop fees and proceed on a straight commission basis." The words "some regularity" are rather ambiguous — how much is "some" and how regular is "regularity"? Much depends on the manuscript in question, I'm certain.

So, unless the writer has credits, he will have to pay for an agency reading. That may mean a rejection slip from the agency. Hey, the author hasn't even gotten to an editor yet and he's getting rejection slips. Is that the way a novice should go? I think not.

In any case, an agent can do very little for the unpublished author. Sure, you can cite a few cases where someone like Frieda Fishbein took Colleen McCullough's *The Thornbirds* (only her second novel) and sold it, turned it into a multi-million dollar product and made both of them rich, but those are one-in-a-million situations. Go with what works. Sell your own stuff to the smaller markets first. Work up to the big markets and *then* look for an agent to negotiate for you.

There is one thing an agent can't do for you. An

agent can't sell a bad manuscript. If you've become frustrated by rejection slip after rejection slip and feel you could do better with a good agent, and you decide to pay the fee for a reading to see what it brings, it will probably just bring another rejection slip.

If you do follow the better path and send your work to the smaller markets, get some credits behind you and grow with your experience, then you will be establishing something for which an agent can respect you and your work. He can then "sell" you to publishers, editors and screenplay producers.

That element of respect must be mutual. You must find the work of the agent to your liking, and the personality of that individual should fit your own. Agents, like editors, look for certain criteria in those they represent. You must make a decision about the kind of person you want representing you, too. The two of you should agree on the basics of what you are trying to do with your career.

WHAT TO EXPECT

As an author, you can expect certain things from an agent. First, your contact with your agent should not be one-way. You need not fear asking the agent for credentials, since he will ask for yours. He will expect a biographical sheet and some copies of your earlier writings. Ask him for his bio sheet and some names and phone numbers of his clients. You may wish to talk with them about their relationship with the agent. If he's the professional he should be, he won't object.

The agent expects you to deliver polished, professional manuscripts to him. Since most agents prefer to handle certain types of manuscripts (fiction for some, women's articles for others, how-to's for others, etc.) you are expected to give him the type of material he specializes in. That information will come with the introductory biographical sketch of the agent and the agency.

You can expect the agent to read the manuscript, research the market, send the manuscript out to the proper editor and wait for a response. Hey, you can do that, right? I suppose you can, but will you? Will you really research the market to see where your best potential lies? Can you keep abreast of the ebb and flow of the publishing tides so that you'll send your manuscript to the right publisher at the right time?

Since the agent studies the market for a living, it seems right that he would have a better grip on what's happening in the publishing world, and he does. The agent may have the inside scoop on the fact that a book publisher has just fired its editor and replaced him with one who has an eye for romance, whereas the former editor liked high adventure. Since the new editor has taken over, the slant of the publishing firm is likely to change. As an author, you can't know about editorial changes as quickly as a good agent can. Without an agent, you could send your high-adventure novel to the publishing company and receive a form rejection slip, then wonder why. A good agent could save you those headaches.

THE AGENT AS EDITOR

An agent is not normally an editor. Many times, agents don't write *or* edit. Agents who negotiate contracts for football players don't normally play in the NFL either, but they know the business end of big-time football. So, an agent may not write or edit, but he may make the difference between an author's receiving a check or not.

Many agents have never written anything, or if they have, they haven't been able to get their work published. If that's the case, then how can an agent help a writer who *has* written and sold some of his own stuff? Well, there's an old axiom: Those who can't do, teach. As absurd as that seems, it's true many times. Even if an agent can't write or edit, when he reads a manuscript he can tell whether it will sell or not. How? It's some instinct (talent) he has which tells him one manuscript is a winner while another one is a loser. So, don't expect the agent to read your manuscript and edit it, correct the flaws and send it to a typist to have it "fixed" for you. He won't do it.

Why then do you want an agent? Some authors simply cannot function by themselves. They go into a room to type and some mysterious thing called "writer's block" hits them and they say they can't keep writing. They walk around and mope all over the house and will not sit down at the typewriter and hit the keys. They call their agent in New York or Los Angeles and tell him their woes. After about twenty minutes of spilling their guts, the agent gives them a verbal kick in the pants and tells them to get back to work. Sometimes the authors who need a swift kick have an agent for that purpose. Some authors need the agent for *that* more than marketing work. It's typing out the prose that's the tough part for them.

THE THIRD VOICE

Another good reason for getting an agent is simply to have a third voice. If someone is trying to sell himself, it's tough to tell another party how good he really is. He needs a third voice. That's the reason so many advertisers use quotes from satisfied customers. It's the old ploy, "If you don't believe me, listen to what Mrs. Jones has to say about our product." When Mrs. Jones begins to expound on the virtues of the product, something happens to the listener and he begins to believe the product is really good.

So, when the editor reads the agent's report on the manuscript, he sees it with a different slant. Sure, the agent has something at stake too, but there is still something different about having someone else tell the editor how good your work is. It sells much more easily (if it has salability at all).

An agent can do a lot of good for an author if the author and the agent have an understanding of what the author wants to accomplish. But an agent can destroy the efforts of an author if the two of them are going in different directions. Misunderstanding and confusion may result.

Working with an agent is like being married. There must be harmony in direction and goals.

THE AGENT -123

CHAPTER ELEVEN

The Great "Come-On"

I have an acquaintance who once wrote a story. His wife encouraged him to send it to a publisher. After being turned down, she pushed him to keep it going. Finally, after several publishers turned it down with form rejection slips and no comments, his discouragement filtered into his wife's attitude too.

After months of letting the manuscript "cool," the couple sat looking through one of the writing trade magazines. Suddenly, one of the big ads jumped off the page and got a stranglehold on both of them. The ad told them their manuscript would be read *"Free."* Of course, they figured they could find out if the thing had any potential. The ad seemed to scream out, "I'm your answer!" So they responded.

Within two weeks a letter arrived, stating that the agency, whose ad had been so seductive, had received the manuscript. The letter went something like this:

> Dear Author:
> This agency has received your manuscript, *Wandering Ukelele Player,* and has recorded same. Copies are being processed and distributed to our editors for reading. We will then have a meeting of the board, at which time, we will be in touch with you.
> Very truly,
>
> Literary Agency
>
> P.S. I don't normally do this, but I took a quick glance at the manuscript you've sent us, and I'm wondering why you haven't sent it directly to a publisher. With my hasty once-over, I can see enough merit to warrant your sending it directly to a major house. I'm looking forward to keeping an eye on its progress.
>
> Agency President

Well, when my buddy got this letter, he called me right away. I hardly had a chance to say, "Hello."

"Wow!" was bashed against my eardrum by this ecstatic man. "Guess what!" I couldn't guess, so he told me what had happened. He read and reread the letter to me, adding innumerable exclamations between readings. I could also hear his wife in the

background, cheering him on.
About a week later, he received another letter from
that agency.

Dear Author:
    You knocked us cold with *Wandering
Ukelele Player!* What a unique story. As I
mentioned in our first letter, I thought a
publisher would just snap it up. Well, after
closer examination, I still feel potential is
there. This is one of those rare pieces an
agent comes across once in a lifetime.
    Mr. Author, I don't know if you've had
any formal training (since there was no
cover sheet), or if your talent is strictly a
gift from above, but we were unanimous in
our judgment of *your potential.*
    Before I go on, I do want to say, there are
areas where you need the aid of experienced
editorial people. Of course, we have a complete staff to handle that for you. And we all
feel this work can't come to a halt, just because of a few mechanical errors.
    Let me say it this way, the rich talent,
though unpolished, may someday be shaped into what just might become another
Hemingway. (One never knows.)
    Please let us know if you would like our
Complete Editorial Comments: Price List.
We're holding your manuscript in our *Wait-
ing-Submission-to-Major-Publishers File.*
(We submit manuscripts we've corrected to
major houses for our authors).
    Please take your time and make a proper
decision.

Sincerely,

Agency President

The day my friend got this letter, he had his reply in the mail within an hour. He called me after returning from the post office. Again my left eardrum vibrated with his "Wow!"

"So read the letter," I stated flatly.

"How'd you know I got another letter?" he asked.

"Your 'Wow!' had that familiar ring to it."

He grunted. "Anyway, listen to this!" He read the letter.

After listening, I realized he was too high on this agency's flattery, to hear my cautioning advice, so I remained silent. His wife was still in the background, cheering more loudly than ever. After hanging up, I shook my head and waited for another week to go by.

The week did go by, and another, and a third had begun, when I called my friend. "Hey," I said, "I haven't heard from you. What's going on?"

"Oh, nuthin' much."

"What about that manuscript, the agency, the letters?"

"Oh," he said. "Yeah, the agency. Well, we've been in touch."

"You sure don't seem very happy."

"Hey, I'm happy," he chuckled. (But it sounded forced.)

"What did they want for correcting your manuscript?"

"Seven-mumble-dollars," he choked, running the words together.

"What was that again?"

"Seven-mumble-dollars."

"Did you send them seven hundred dollars?" I screamed.

"Don't get excited," he laughed. "We knew better than to go for that kind of deal. We just sent them the fee for editorial comment." He laughed again. "Do ya think I'm a nut?"

Well, I didn't want to answer that so I figured he had sent them fifty bucks and said, "At least for fifty bucks you can see if you have something worth doing anything with."

"Yeah," he agreed.

That telephone conversation was the last I heard from my friend for almost two-and-a-half months. Then, one day, I ran into him and his wife at the supermarket. I noticed they waved hurriedly and started down another aisle. I headed them off.

After the normal amenities, I asked, "How's the book coming?"

"Fine," he said.

"Fine," she added. "How's Bobbie?"

"Fine," I said. "Are you doing any good with that agency?"

"Fine," he said.

"Fine," she added again.

"Well, tell me about it."

"Ah — They sent it to Random House, and —" he glanced at his wife.

"Doubleday," she said.

"Oh, yeah," he shook his head, "Doubleday, too. Yep, Doubleday."

"So, you let them correct it, huh?" I remembered the seven hundred dollars, and lifted an eyebrow and waited. They looked at each other.

"Uh-huh," my friend said.

"Listen, call us sometime soon, and we'll discuss

it," his wife broke in. "We have to run now." She began pushing the grocery cart down the aisle. They both followed it closely, saying their goodbyes without looking back.

It was nearly a year later before we had a serious talk and I found out what had been going on. My friends had become victims of the literary con-artist agency. (In the business of words, there are thousands of con games that can be played.) Reread the first and second letters received by this unsuspecting couple, and see if you find any place where they are told they *will* succeed.

Letters like these, are sent out everyday by someone who is playing on the pride of thousands of people who think they have talent "sent from above," and all the agency is doing, is providing the necessary ingredient: "I believe in you." The potential author is soon off to the races. In fact, he would be better off betting on the ponies than playing the word game with these con men. (Either way, he'd lose.)

I finally got my opportunity to sit down and have a nice, long chat with my friends. Here is what I discovered.

"We sent two-hundred-fifty dollars for a 'complete analysis' of our manuscript and general writing skills."

"I thought it was fifty," I said. "You must have gotten the deluxe treatment for two-hundred-fifty dollars."

He bit his lip, and she answered, "Six typewritten pages of 'complete analysis.' We were floating." She looked down to the floor. "Now that we have quit floating and have reread the six pages, we can see it is all flattery and empty words."

He looked at me. "They had given us meaningless

phrases that *seemed* to tell us we were on the verge of having a bestseller."

They both hestitated, so I prodded. "And?" I asked solemnly.

"And, we sent them another four-hundred-fifty bucks," he twisted nervously. "It took care of the expenses of correcting the manuscript to 'make it ready for publication.' " He sighed. "By then, we were hooked. It's like playing the bandits in Vegas."

His wife spoke up. "They kept sending us letters explaining the facts of editing to us, and how they had sent our script to this publishing house, or that one, and the next one might buy it if it just had another change." She paused, smiling. "Each change got more expensive."

I sat there looking at them for a few moments. "Well, should I ask?" I pursed my lips, then added, "Or will my heart be able to stand the shock?"

By then they were relieved to have told me this much and began to laugh at themselves. They looked at each other, then in unison said, "Thirty-four-mumble-dollars."

I grabbed my chest with one hand. "You don't mean it!"

He nodded. "Yup."

I placed my other hand over the first and took a deep breath. "Thirty-four hundred dollars?" I asked. "You really mean you spent thirty-four hundred dollars to get your manuscript published?"

"Nope," he said.

"What do you mean, 'Nope'? You just said you spent thirty-four hundred dollars with that agency!"

"We did," his wife said, "but the book never got published."

This poor couple happen to be one of many thousands of people who need to hear our seminar, where I say, *"Never, never, never pay anyone anything to publish your work or get someone else to publish your work!"* I always go over that three or four times. I add emphasis with each declaration.

Note: As a beginning author, never pay anyone to publish, or represent your work. If it isn't professional enough to have a publishing house pay you, then it isn't good enough at all. Work harder.

A NEW TWIST

There's a new angle on the market today. Publishers have had to come up with this new twist during the recent economic recession. Many companies were losing everything, and those who were surviving were just keeping their heads above financial water.

The survivors began to take another look at their book sales and the manuscripts they had been buying. Since they were having such a tough time, they decided to take the risk out of publishing books by unknown authors. The way they have done that is to publish books with a contract giving them a guarantee that the author will purchase 50% of the initial press run at 60% of the cover price. If the press run is 5000 copies (a normal run), the author is obligated to purchase 2500 copies at 60% of the cover price. If the cover price is $7.95, the author must come up with $11,925. That's a bit much for most writers.

Let's say you do come up with the money. Now you own 2500 copies of your book at a cover price of $7.95. If you could retail them, you'd gross $19,875 for a gross profit of $7950. Notice I said *"if"* you could retail the copies you owned. There is a clause in your contract that prevents you from retailing the books in bookstores. You may display them at personal appearances, speaking engagements, conventions and the like, and sell them at retail during your engagements at those functions, but you *cannot* sell them in stores or to stores.

Since this new twist has appeared, several slick agents have found this "no risk" publishing venture appealing and have decided to jump in on the action. These agents contact a local printer and set up a deal with him to publish some cheap paperbacks for a handsome profit. The agent attempts to sell the manuscript for the novice author, but doesn't try very hard. After telling the author it has been turned down by several houses, the agent suggests that he give it a try at Positive Press (fictitious name). He says he understands that the publisher at Positive Press will publish this author's book if the author will buy half of the first run. The agent encourages the author to do so and says, "I'll even forfeit my 10% commission to help you get started." Of course, he's going to get his cut from the overpriced printer. *This is one reason the novice writer must be very careful in choosing an agent.*

LEGITIMATE AGENCIES

What about the legitimate agencies like Scott Meredith's and Frieda Fishbein's and many others? What can they do for the author who has made a beginning?

Any legitimate agency can and will guide the careers of its authors, if those authors are willing to take advice. The agent knows good writing when he sees it, and he knows rotten prose when he reads it. He can guide the writing, the contracting, the financial direction and the public life of the writer. In fact, some "big name" authors don't do *anything* without the advice of their agents.

In his book, *Writing To Sell*, Scott Meredith says, "Generally speaking, an agent who has many established professionals among his clients is bound to be honest and reliable — because writers pass the word around quickly when an agent is shady, and the shady agent's list quickly dissolves or never gets built up. There's one way to find out about an agent's clients, incidently: write and ask him." (*Writing To Sell*, Scott Mcredith, Harper & Row, New York, NY, Copyright 1974.)

Scott Meredith says he has prodded authors, led authors, forced authors and even loaned money to some authors to bring them out of the mental dilemma of writer's block. But even good agents who enhance the careers of their professional clients can't do much for the amateur writer. Each must pay the dues of experience, study and hard work.

CHAPTER TWELVE

Where to Begin and What to Do

Now that you know what you want to write, have a feel for the industry and understand agents, it's time to go to work at the craft of writing.

Let's say you've gone down to your local library and researched the publishing company, discovering its approach, slant and style. You know exactly what kind of material the editor of your choice is looking for and you know you can provide it. When you sit down at your typewriter, you make a synopsis of your over-all manuscript and design an extensive outline. Having done all this, you are ready to write.

Since you're working on your first draft of this proposed book, you decide to use inexpensive paper. That's good, but it also provides a psychological pitfall that you need to avoid. When you roll a cheap piece of paper into your typewriter, you may rationalize that the first draft can be less than your best work. *After all, you think, it's only the first draft. Nobody's going to see it.* WRONG! *You're* going to see it, and you're going to use it as the foundation on which you will build the entire work. If you do anything less than your best, you'll be building on a faulty foundation. Always be careful to write with the idea of giving your best performance.

All right, you feed an inexpensive sheet of paper into the roller. Some authors use that yellowish newsprint as first-draft paper. I prefer a cheap white paper (I suppose the white paper is my psychological hedge against sloppy writing). In any case, the size must be 8½" x 11" so that you'll have the "feel" of the final manuscript's length when you've finished your first draft.

You'll want to use a better grade of sixteen-pound bond for your final draft. It should have a plain finish and 25% rag content. Never use 11" x 14", or any size other than 8½" x 11". Don't use colored paper, onionskin or erasable bond. Remember, you want your manuscript to look as professional as you can possibly make it. So, think of the first page as a business letter of sorts which presents an image of you and your work.

Even your first draft should look good. Using a typewriter with clean keys is imperative. If you allow the keys to collect bits of ribbon and ink, over a period of time you'll begin to overlook the general appearance of your work and allow smudges on the page and o's without holes to mar its professionalism. So, constantly check and clean the keys to make certain your work is crisp and neat.

Always double-space your work. Remember, even if you quote paragraphs from other published books or articles in your manuscript, always type them out and double-space to fit the quoted material in with the overall manuscript. If you wish that portion of the copy to stand out, simply indent five extra spaces on each line.

If you don't have a typewriter, you can possibly rent time on one at your local library. Some libraries have special typing rooms sealed off from the rest of the library. There is never any need to send handwritten material to an editor. In fact, most editors won't even read manuscripts written in longhand or printed with a pen or pencil.

Using both sides of the paper is *verboten*. In fact, the use of carbon paper should be limited. Carbon paper is fine for some projects, but manuscript writing is not one of them. If the carbon paper is put into the machine backward, it looks as though you've typed on both sides of the paper and it really smudges type on the front side only.

Always keep a copy of work you send to a publisher.

BEGIN NOW

As you type your manuscript, the first thing you want to do is make certain each page is clearly numbered so there will be no confusion for you (when editing) or for the editing when reading your work. Identify your work by typing your name in the upper left corner of the first page. Type your address directly below that (single-spaced), then below that put your city, state and *ZIP* code. You may also type your phone number or social security number. After you've done that, roll the paper through the roller until both ends of the paper meet. You will then be typing just above the center of the page. Now determine the length of your title, center it and type it, with your byline centered two spaces below.

Roll the paper down four spaces, indent five spaces from the left margin and begin your manuscript. Be certain to double-space between lines. Make sure you have plenty of margin all around.

GOING ON

After you have finished your first draft of the manuscript, read it aloud, editing as you go. After you have done all you can to improve it with editorial markings, retype the entire manuscript.

Now that you've rewritten it, go over it another time, editing again. Believe me, you'll find plenty to edit. Even if you've done a good job on the first editing, and even if you caught a lot of stuff in the retyping, you'll still find more ways to improve it.

When the second editing is finished and you've actually cut parts out, sweated over it and retyped the entire manuscript once again, I suggest you then find someone (a spouse, perhaps) who will listen as you read it aloud. Now, the person who is listening is not usually a professional author, editor or literature critic, but that isn't the purpose of using a second person anyway. The reason for reading it to someone else is that, in the reading, you will see errors which stall the smooth effect you're looking for. You'll be able to stop and make the necessary corrections right in the middle of the reading. Try it and see. It works. You'll wind up polishing your work to a fine gloss.

AT LAST

So now you have edited and rewritten until you can't do it again. You're slumped in your chair, exhausted. You've had it with this story, and you're going to send it out even if it isn't perfect. If it has come down to that after many editings and rewritings, fine. But if you're giving in after rewriting it only once or twice, you're probably in for a pile of rejections in the weeks to come.

But let's say you have edited and rewritten extensively, and know your manuscript is ready. Okay, you can send it out now. Check your list of editors who accept unsolicited manuscripts of the type you've written (provided you didn't have to query them first), then get out your card file and create a record of where you will send it. Simply write the name of the manuscript with the number of words (or pages) at the top of the card, along with the date it was completed. Under that, put the name of the publisher and publication along with the editor's name. Under that, write the address for easy reference.

Send a good copy, on bond paper, to the editor. If you've submitted a query and the editor sent a favorable response, you will want to remind him with a short cover letter. Thank him for his interest in the piece you've designed for his magazine, publishing house, etc. If you didn't send a query and are submitting the piece as unsolicited material, be certain to submit a short cover letter stating that you've studied the editor's output lately and have designed this piece for his magazine, publishing house, etc. The cover letter must be brief and should be single-spaced. Don't go into long explanations about how you had to do this or that, or that your Aunt Elizabeth or Uncle Ralph loved this final draft. Also, you may wish to put the rights you are offering in the upper right corner of the first page. If you've done your homework you already know what rights the editor normally buys.

You may wish to put a blank cover sheet on the top and bottom of the manuscript to keep it fresh while it's being handled. Use a paper clip if the manuscript is less than thirty pages; if not, you may wish to have a piece of cardboard cut to size and put it over the manuscript, holding it in place with rubber bands.

Your manuscript will get better treatment by a publishing house if you don't make it stand out by pasting stickers on the envelope or using a brightly-colored envelope, or by sending an envelope with an odd shape or size. The editors know those pieces come from amateurs and treat them as such. The more professional your manuscript looks, the better your chances of getting a positive reading. Some editors actually pick out the odd-looking envelopes and quickly dispense with them by attaching a rejection slip and sending them back to the front desk. Others toss them in the corner and forget them for weeks.

Place a self-addressed, stamped envelope inside the mailing envelope, but don't seal it yet.

At the post office, weigh your manuscript to be sure there is enough postage on the envelope. You'll want to be certain to have sufficient postage on your SASE.

Don't register it. Don't insure it. Don't ask that an editor sign for a return receipt. There is no need to do anything except mail the piece. You may choose to mail it first class, third class or special fourth class, depending on your economic status.

Even though editors say, "Simultaneous submissions OK," sending your manuscript to more than one editor at a time is not a good practice. Editors take a dim view of responding positively to a manuscript only to be told it's been purchased by someone else, and they may decline to read your work again.

If you follow these instructions, you won't need an agent. You can afford the time and effort to do what it takes to get all the necessary information. You need the experience anyway. You need to stay in tune with the market news. If you subscribe to any of the three national writing magazines, *The Writer*, *Writer's Digest* or *The Christian Writer*, you'll get the market news. Obviously, *The Christian Writer* is slanted toward the inspirational market, *The Writer* and *Writer's Digest* appeal to the general writing audience.

I WAITED SIX MONTHS

That brings us to the waiting period. Normally, the writer's guidelines will give you an indication of the time it usually takes for the editor to respond to your submission. If the "gestation period" is not listed, a good rule of thumb is to wait about ten weeks before you write to ask about your work.

I sent my first novel, *Thieves*, to a publisher and waited for the allotted ten weeks, then thought I'd give it a couple more. Finally, after about fourteen weeks, I wrote to the editor. She responded with a positive maybe. That didn't help me, but I knew they were working on it and I was happy about that. After another six weeks, I had to give them a call. I just couldn't stand any more waiting — it had been a full twenty weeks since I'd seen my manuscript, and I was getting itchy. Well, I called to prod the editor. She then pushed the editorial board for a decision. Another couple of weeks went by and I was frustrated enough to give up. Finally, after a total of twenty-six weeks, I received a call from the editor and heard her say, "Mr. Noton, we've decided to accept your novel." It came out in hardcover first. After that, it was released in trade paperback. Now it's out in mass paperback and I've signed a major motion picture deal on it, so it was worth the wait.

Just have patience (up to a point). Then, if you must, write or call. Writing a simple inquiry is best. Editors don't like calls from authors. They usually don't result in enough information for the author anyway.

DO IT ALL YOURSELF

Until you *can't* do it all yourself, do it all yourself. When the day comes that you can't do it all, an agent will be waiting with open arms. Until then, the better agents probably can't and won't do much to improve your acceptance ratio. But once you become rich and famous from your writings, an agent may be able to negotiate better contracts for you, big advances against bigger royalties, or some side benefits you couldn't have gotten for yourself.

You write, *you* research, *you* outline, *you* study the markets, *you* send the manuscript, *you* receive the acceptance or rejection and *you* spend all the money you get from dispensing your blood, sweat and tears.

You *can* get your foot in the editorial door if you apply these principles.